CW01648984

MURRAY WALKER'S

GRAND PRIX CHALLENGE

STUART SYKES & CHARLES BALCHIN

FIRST FROST PUBLISHING

PUBLISHER'S NOTES

Murray Walker's Grand Prix Challenge was conceived over dinner at a restaurant on the water's edge of Lake Como, the night before the Italian Grand Prix of 1988. Present were Murray Walker, Charles Balchin, and Roger Chown — publisher of First Frost's motor racing books. The idea, like all good ones, stemmed from an observation that Grand Prix fans not only enthuse about their love, but know so much about it; on the Page and Moy bus to Monza that morning, one Simon — an aficionado if ever there was one — had startled the Publisher with his amazing recall, not of races he had attended which was impressive enough, but of those he had not even been out of nappies to 'experience'. Charles Balchin added the meal's missing ingredient, the *concept* of a Grand Prix Challenge, and the book was born.

Stuart Sykes, now Editor of *Prix Editions International* magazine and another with encyclopaedic knowledge of Grand Prix racing was the obvious partner and together the three main protagonists — the 'voice,' the TV producer, and the F1 magazine expert — constructed the book. For the Publisher, already depth-charged by their wisdom, the process was simple enough . . . in theory; just produce the book. But . . . how was it to be? How many times could the inventors tease and essay? How should it work as a book? It was really the good Doctor Sykes who gave this book its form and for better or for worse, the now 'wedded' partners acquiesced with monstrous enthusiasm.

The result follows. The aim is simple enough. The authors have, within the framework of a sixteen-race series of Grand Prix races, devised questions of varying levels of difficulty. They have assigned the questions in such a way that hopefully *anyone* interested can enjoy the book, but have taken account too, of the enormous knowledge which exists 'outside' the professional spheres of journalism in motor sport.

Some of the questions do in some ways, get repeated although hopefully with different slants — this is deliberate. The pictures used are all drawn from the wonderful archive collection at LAT Photographic — to them, all concerned in the project owe a big debt, and no doubt a small cheque!

It is possible you will disagree with an answer and be able to 'prove' it, e.g., Who *was* the youngest winner of a World Championship Grand Prix Event. But with careful reading you may also decide that 'strictly speaking' the answer given is right. We hope so.

Producing any book is great fun and hard work. The Publishers of *Murray Walker's Grand Prix Challenge* would like to thank the following:

The Marlboro Grand Prix Guide.
The Guinness Book of Records.
The Grand Prix Data Book 1989.
Murray Walker's Grand Prix Year, vols 1, 2 and 3.
BBC Television.
Longines
The restaurant at Lake Como — name not recalled.
Tim Collings for verifying our questions and answers.
Linda Blakemore and Eve White for their design.
Jim Brooks and the Clifford Frost Ltd team.
FISA, FIA and FOCA.
The authors of countless Grand Prix books.
The authors for their lunatic devotion.
All the men and women, who have since 1950 given the enthusiasts of Grand Prix racing, the statistics, the miracles and the sheer skills which have made this project possible.
Allsport and John Townsend for additional photographs.

ROGER CHOWN, November 1989.

Published by First Formula Publishing, an imprint of First Frost Ltd

First published 1989
ISBN 1 870066 18 9
Edited by Roger Chown Typeset, printed and produced by Clifford Frost Ltd
Reproduction by Sinclair Graphics

CONTENTS

WARM-UP LAP — JUST TESTING?!

1 Who was world Drivers' Champion in 1968?

2 Who preceded him? Was it (a) Jack Brabham (b) Dennis Hulme or (c) Jacky Stewart.

3 Who is this?

(a) Murray Walker

(b) James Hunt

(c) Jean Marie Balestre.

4 Which of the following UK magazines is published weekly?

(a) Autosport (b) Motoring News (c) The Sun (d) Prix Editions International.

5 Which French-engined car gave Team Williams victory in Canada in 1989?

6 Which Italian engine used a V12 configuration during 1989, apart from Ferrari?

7 When was the last Grand Prix of Europe? Was it; (a) 1985 (b) 1958 (c) 1598.

8 Who is the only knight in Grand Prix's shining armour?

9 Who was the senior producer of BBC TV's Grand Prix programme in 1989?

10 Which driver in *Murray Walker's Grand Prix Year volume 3* was singled out for his 'special' performances in 1989? Was it;

(a) Pierluigi Martini (b) Jean Alesi (c) Gabriele Tarquini.

For answers see page 8.

WORDS AND PICTURES

FROM 'THE CHALLENGE TEAM'

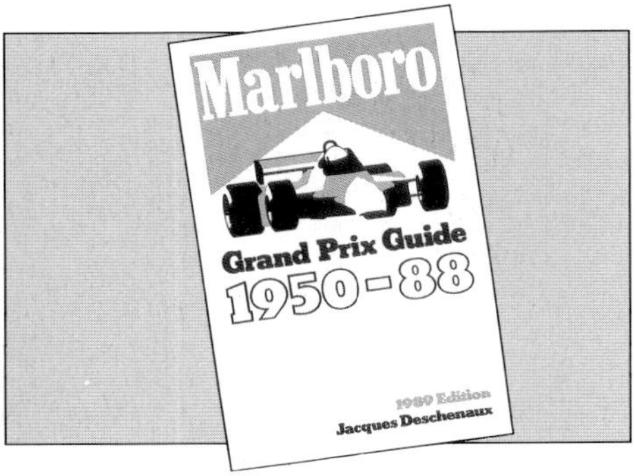

'I couldn't put it down.'
— *Editor,* Murray Walker's Grand Prix Challenge.

'I took it to bed every night for six weeks.'
— *Author Charles Balchin.*

'I know!'
— *Girlfriend of author Charles Balchin.*

'It's got almost as many notes as I have!'
— *Murray Walker.*

'A remarkable record' — Motoring News.

'Thanks for the memories' — *Editor of* Murray Walker's Grand Prix Challenge.

'Didn't I pay *last* time?' — *Charles Balchin, Author, and ex-producer BBC TV Grand Prix programme speaking to Murray Walker.*

'Who does the other voice, Murray?' — *Stuart Sykes, author.*

'I am totally exhausted' — *Charles Balchin to Stuart Sykes.*

'Motor Racing is fun' — *Ron Dennis.*

'I knew it would come in handy' — *Editor,* Murray Walker's Grand Prix Year.

'I'm just glad I didn't have to type it' — *PA to Stuart Sykes, author.*

'Positively therapeutic . . . what am I saying!!' — *Stuart Sykes, author.*

'No help at all — but the pictures are fabulous' — *Stuart Sykes, author.*

'Hell on earth' — *Anon.*

'An outrageous offering' — Daily Mail.

Q: Who wrote 'the only winner is the first one to pass the Chequered Flag!' Ayrton Senna?
A: Just teasing of course. Only FISA *always* know the real winner.

Q: Who said 'I've never really enjoyed a real Grand Prix book, but I've certainly featured in a few?' Was it (a) Nigel Mansell, (b) Andrea De Cesaris or (c) Jean Marie Balestre?
A: On a postcard, please.

Q: Should we start on another Grand Prix Challenge?
A: 'No!!!' (a choral response from Stuart Sykes and Charles Balchin) 'shoot the editor' . . . came the reply.

ANSWERS TO WARM-UP QUESTIONS

1 Graham Hill.

2 Denis Hulme. But of course you noted the two deliberate spelling mistakes? Well, didn't you? Denis is spelled with one *N* and *Jacky* Stewart is of course spelled Jackie.

3 Murray Walker.

4 (a) and (b). *The Sun* is not weekly, and (d) so we hear from the Editor, is a monthly from 1990.

5 Renault.

6 Lamborghini.

7 1985. In 1598 the 'Grand Prix of Europe' was probably Germany!

8 Sir Jack Brabham (wouldn't it be good to have more).

9 Jim Reside.

10 Pierluigi Martini.

THE RULES

When the book was originally conceived, it was felt that the 'Challenge' should embrace both the 'team' idea, and the more straightforward notion of a single enthusiast simply testing his or her own knowledge.

To assist in the enjoyment of the book we devised a nominal scoring system which you may care to use as follows:

First Qualifying — for each correct answer score one point.

Second Qualifying — for each correct answer score one point.

In a 'team' game, anyone scoring less than six points fails to qualify for the grid, i.e., Race Day questions.

Race Day — to get a finish overall, at least four Race Day questions have to be answered correctly at a scoring level of two points each. These should, of course, be added to the points attained in Qualifying sessions, as should Pit Stop questions — all of which are deliberately harder and therefore, we suggest, deserving of five points. To add to the sense of realism, you could break Race Day questions and insert one or more of the Pit Stop sections. A 'quick pit stop' could 'turn' the final result of the 'race'.

To 'tune' your own enjoyment please feel free to alter the system as fits your needs, but . . . whatever system you devise, remember that we have devised these rules as 'fun' — it may be a serious business and who knows money could change hands but it is a sport and the spirit of this enterprise is entertainment not GCSE Motor Racing.

Round One faces you — anyone getting the first question wrong should be given a six-wheel Skoda with a workshop manual written by Jean-Marie Balestre!

BRAZIL

FIRST QUALIFYING

1 What does the term 'Grand Prix' mean?

5 Which is the longest circuit drivers faced in 1989?

▲

2 It's a Brabham. It's 1963. Which American is driving?

3 Jim Clark won 25 times but came second only once. True or false?

▼

4 Who is the most successful British driver ever?

6 What was born in 1977 and died in 1988?

7 Which three drivers are BBC Sports Personality of the Year award winners?

8 How was the 1975 British GP a notable first?

▼

9 Juan Manuel Fangio started the 1954 season with Maserati, but to which other team was he contracted?

10 Who had three separate spells with Ferrari in the Fifties?

11 When did a British car finally win the British GP?

12 In what year did Mike Hawthorn become World Champion?

13 When did Brands Hatch first host the British GP? 1964? 1967? 1969?

14 Who was the first winner at Brands Hatch?

15 Two milestones marked the 1967 Dutch GP: what were they?

16 Who was the first Frenchman to win the World Championship?

SECOND QUALIFYING

▲

1 In what car did Jochen Rindt win the World Championship?

2 Who won his first title in 1972?

3 Where did the great Gilles Villeneuve win his last race?

4 Which car won four races in 1954 and five the following year?

5 When did Porsche enter their last F1 race: 1962/64/66?

6 There has been one Kiwi World Champion: who, when?

7 Which circuit staged the European GP in 1952, 1958 and 1965?

8 When did Aintree first stage the British GP: 1955/57/59?

9 Who was runner-up in the Drivers' Championship in 1963-64-65?

10 Who was World Champion in an Alfa Romeo 158?

11 What does the yellow flag signify to the driver?

12 In the days of national racing colours, what were Germany's?

13 New Zealander . . . Came to Europe in 1958 to join Jack Brabham's GP team . . . Won in his own right in 1968: Who?

14 Mike Hawthorn won Grands Prix in only one make of car: true or false?

15 Which famous circuit hosted a World Championship GP for the first ten years — and never again?

16 At which World Championship venue was the RenCen a dominant feature?

▼

RACE DAY

▲

1 Michele Alboreto was back with Tyrrell in '89 after how many races with Ferrari? 70, 80 or 90.

2 Which of the current teams (to the end of 1989) has the longest unchanged driver combination?

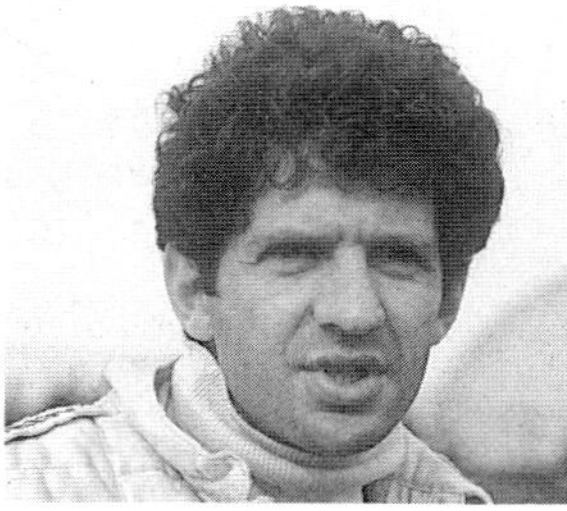

▲

◀ ◀ *3* These three men were rated at 3/1, 9/2 and 6/1 respectively for the title in one season. Which, and who are they?

4 Who became BRM's third driver alongside Jean-Pierre Beltoise and Clay Regazzoni in 1972?

▲

5 Who led the Drivers' Championship going into the final round at Kyalami in 1983?

6 What race number is associated with Stirling Moss?

7 On his return to Grand Prix racing after 'retirement', where did Niki Lauda celebrate his first victory?

8 How did Bruno Giacomelli and Eliseo Salazar embarrass each other at the 1982 Belgian GP?

9 True or false? In 1979 Gilles Villeneuve became the first man to win the Canadian and USA West GPs in one season.

10 Only once, in 1964, did Zeltweg host the Austrian GP. Who won?

11 Which former team owner became a junior Environment Minister?

12 Who retired from Grand Prix racing after the 1958 French GP?

13 What was significant about Jackie Stewart's 1973 Dutch GP victory?

14 Taking the winner's average speed as guide, what is the fastest circuit ever used?

15 Who were the first turbo-charged Constructors' Champions?

16 Who announced his retirement at the 1979 Canadian GP?

PIT STOP (1):

BRAZIL

1 Name the circuit on which the Brazilian GP is run.

▼

2 What was it previously called?

3 Where else has the Brazilian round been held?

▼

4 Which driver has won the Brazilian GP most often?

5 Which Brazilian driver scored his only GP win in Brazil?

6 Who won the first Brazilian GP?

7 Only three drivers have claimed pole position in Brazil twice: who are they?

8 Three teams share the highest number of victories in Brazil. How many, and which teams?

PIT STOP (2):

A YEAR IN FORMULA ONE: 1950

1 The very first World Championship winner. How many races were there altogether?

▼

2 At which race was the field reduced from 19 to 9 cars within the first lap?

3 Son of a famous Ferrari driver . . . Drove for Ferrari . . . The main threat to Alfa-Romeo domination: who was he?

4 What was significant about the new Ferrari at the Belgian race that year?

5 Which driver retired twice from the Italian GP?

6 Which team made an ignominious start to the World Championship when its entry broke down on the starting grid?

7 The Monaco race of that year is still the slowest on record. True or false?

8 Which team took six cars to the French GP but saw them all eliminated within 15 laps?

PIT STOP (3):

TEAM TALK: BRABHAM

1 Which was Brabham's first full Championship season?

2 Who were the drivers then?

3 How many Grands Prix did Nelson Piquet win for them?

▼

4 Brabham were never World Constructors' Champions when Piquet drove for the team. True or false?

5 When was a Brabham first on pole?

6 Who was the New Zealander who co-founded the team with Jack Brabham?

7 What was the designation of Gordon Murray's first fully-fledged Brabham design?

8 Who was the first Englishman to drive for Brabham?

PIT STOP (4):

THE WORLD CHAMPIONS (1)

1 Who was the first driver to win the title in a turbo-charged car?

2 Scotland has had a ▶ World Champion more often than England. True or false?

3 Who was the last Ferrari driver to claim the title?

▼

4 This man and three others have retained the title. Who are they?

5 Which World Champion was nicknamed 'The Rat'?

6 For how many teams ▶ did James Hunt drive?

7 Name two World Champions who have raced in Grands Prix against their own brothers.

8 What unique and sad distinction fell to Jochen Rindt?

RESULTS

FIRST QUALIFYING

1 Great Prize.
2 Dan Gurney.
3 True — German GP 1963.
4 Jackie Stewart with 27 wins.
5 Spa-Francorchamps at 4.31 miles/6.94 kms.
6 Turbocharging
7 Stirling Moss 1961, Jackie Stewart 1973, Nigel Mansell 1986.
8 The race itself was sponsored by John Player.
9 Mercedes.
10 Mike Hawthorn.
11 1957 — Brooks/Moss in a Vanwall.
12 1958.
13 1964.
14 Jim Clark (Lotus).
15 First victory for both the Ford-Cosworth DFV and Lotus 49.
16 Alain Prost in 1985.

SECOND QUALIFYING

1 Lotus 72.
2 Emerson Fittipaldi.
3 Spanish GP 1981.
4 Mercedes-Benz.
5 1962.
6 Denny Hulme, 1967.
7 Spa-Francorchamps in Belgium.
8 1955.
9 Graham Hill.
10 Giuseppe Farina — the first ever in 1950.
11 Do not overtake.
12 All white.
13 Bruce McLaren.
14 True: his three wins were all for Ferrari.
15 Indianapolis.
16 The Renaissance Center is the symbol of Detroit's urban renewal.

RACE ONE

1 Eighty.
2 Arrows — Cheever and Warwick came together for 1987.
3 1979: Mario Andretti, Jody Scheckter and Carlos Reutemann.
4 Niki Lauda.
5 Alain Prost — but Nelson Piquet took the title.
6 Seven.
7 Long Beach, 1982.
8 They came together on the parade lap and did not start.
9 False: Carlos Reutemann did it the year before.
10 Lorenzo Bandini, Ferrari.
11 Lord Hesketh.
12 Juan Manuel Fangio.
13 It was his 26th — one more than the record held by Jim Clark.
14 Monza — 150.75 mph in 1971.
15 Ferrari.
16 Niki Lauda — 'tired of driving round and round in circles'.

PIT STOP (1):

BRAZIL

1 Autodromo Nelson Piquet.
2 Jacarepagua.
3 Interlagos — the last race there was in 1980.
4 Alain Prost: five victories to 1988.
5 Carlos Pace: 1975, Brabham.
6 Emerson Fittipaldi: 1973, Lotus.
7 Ronnie Peterson: 1973 and 1978; James Hunt: 1976 and 1977; and Ayrton Senna: 1988 and 1989.
8 Four: Lotus, McLaren and Ferrari.

PIT STOP (2):

A YEAR IN F1 1950

1 Seven — including Indianapolis.
2 Monaco — Farina skidded on seawater at Tabac Corner.
3 Alberto Ascari, son of Antonio.
4 It was the first Ferrari without super-charging.
5 Juan Manuel Fangio (Alfa Romeo), who took over Taruffi's car when his own expired but enjoyed no better luck with it.
6 BRM at Silverstone.
7 True: the average speed of 61.33 mph is by far the slowest.
8 Maserati.

PIT STOP (3):

TEAM TALK: BRABHAM

1 1963.
2 Jack Brabham and Dan Gurney.
3 13.
4 True.
5 Dutch GP 1964 (Gurney).
6 Ron Tauranac.
7 BT42 (1973).
8 Piers Courage in 1969.

PIT STOP (4):

THE WORLD CHAMPIONS (1)

1 Nelson Piquet, Brabham 1983.
2 False: five each (Clark ×2; Stewart ×3; Hawthorn, Hill ×2; Surtees, Hunt).
3 Jody Scheckter in 1979.
4 Alberto Ascari (1952-53); Juan Manuel Fangio (1954-55-56-57); Jack Brabham (1959-60); Alain Prost (1985-86).
5 Niki Lauda.
6 Four: March, Hesketh, McLaren, Wolf.
7 Emerson Fittipaldi (Wilson) and Jody Scheckter (Ian).
8 He was the only posthumous World Champion (1970).

SCORE		
1st QUAL.		
2nd QUAL.		
RACE		
PITSTOP (1)		
PITSTOP (2)		
PITSTOP (3)		
PITSTOP (4)		
TOTAL		

SAN MARINO

FIRST QUALIFYING

1 Who had his first GP win in Las Vegas in 1982, and his last in Germany in 1985?

2 True or False? Satoru Nakajima is the only Japanese driver to have collected World Championship points.

▼

6 Who made his debut in a Brabham in the very last race they appeared in before their one year absence?

7 Which driver was sacked from the Minardi team half way through 1988?

11 What record do Jim Clark, Alain Prost and Ayrton Senna share?

12 Which local hero made his debut in the 1988 Japanese GP?

13 1989 team-mates Cheever and Warwick share an unenviable record. What is it?

3 Which current driver scored his first points in only his second drive in a Tyrrell in Australia in 1985?

4 Of the 1989 driver line up who has had more teams than anyone else?

5 Who was the first British driver since James Hunt to gain a Top 3 Podium place?

8 Which current driver was charged with manslaughter in 1978 after Ronnie Peterson's death?

9 In his long career Riccardo Patrese has posted two wins, both with one team. Which one?

10 For how many teams has Alain Prost driven to the end of 1989?

14 Who was the last Frenchman to win the French GP in a French car?

15 In 1982 Keke Rosberg won only one race, the Swiss GP on the way to the title. Where was it?

16 True or false? No one has yet won a GP at an average speed of over 150 mph.

SECOND QUALIFYING

▲

1 True or false? In 1982 the USA hosted three GPs.

2 Of the 1988 circuits which two featured a tunnel?

3 True or false? Less than a second separated the first five at the 1971 Italian GP.

4 Which British driver had his first win in the same year that James Hunt became champion?

5 True or false? Nelson Piquet snatched all three of his titles in the last race of the season.

6 Which two former World Champions had their last races at the 1986 Australian GP?

7 True or false? The first ever Championship Brazil GP was won by a Brazilian.

8 True or false? The 1964 championship wasn't decided till the last lap of the last race.

9 Which was the first South American country to stage a Championship GP. Was it Brazil or Argentina?

10 What engine did Brabham, Benetton and Arrows all share in 1986?

11 In which race in 1988 did Alain Prost drive down the inside of Ayrton Senna into the first corner, only to slide wide and allow Senna back into the lead?

12 Why did Nigel Mansell miss a few races in 1988?

▼

13 Who is the best paid racing driver of all time?

14 Where did Arrows achieve their best result of 1988?

15 Who was the first World Champion on Goodyear tyres. Was it Jack Brabham, Jackie Stewart or Niki Lauda?

16 Which designer is known as 'The Duke'?

RACE DAY

1 Who had a Swiss flag emblazoned on his helmet?

2 The 1961 Dutch GP saw a unique event. What?

▼

3 Of the races on the 1988 calendar only four have always been held on the same track. Which ones?

4 Where and when did Mike Hawthorn drive his last race?

5 What did Jack Brabham do at the 1960 British GP which caused him to be ticked off by officials?

6 Who was trapped in his car for over an hour at the 1982 German GP?

7 In what year was in-race refuelling last seen?

8 Who was the 'Farnham Flyer'?

9 Which two drivers shared a Vanwall to victory in the 1957 British GP?

10 Which team took a 1-2-3-4 at the 1955 British GP?

11 Which team used an aircraft aerodynamicist to improve their car?

12 Who was the first British driver to win two GPs in a row?

13 Which 1980 GP was won by Alan Jones, but because of a row between the sport's governing bodies did not count to the title?

14 Which driver habitually drove with a back to front tweed cap?

15 In which year were all skirts banned from F1 racing cars?

16 How many wins in succession did Alberto Ascari score in 1952?

▼

PIT STOP (1):

SAN MARINO

1 In which year did Imola stage the Italian GP?

2 After whom is the Imola circuit named?

3 Only one section of the Imola circuit bears a driver's name. Which?

4 Which well-known team staged its return to Grand Prix racing at Imola in 1987?

5 Which two drivers have won the San Marino GP for Ferrari?

6 What was unusual about the 1982 San Marino race?

7 Name the first British driver to score a point at Imola?

8 Which Italian driver scored one of his only two Grand Prix victories at Imola in 1985?

PIT STOP (2):

A YEAR IN FORMULA ONE: 1963

1 What was unique about Jim Clark's Championship success?

2 Who, at the Belgian GP, was the youngest-ever entrant in a World Championship race?

3 What was significant about John Surtees' German GP victory?

4 Who lost his points in France after being push-started?

5 What error caused chaos at the start of the French GP?

6 Which team entered for the British GP but withdrew after a disappointing practice?

7 Which Italian announced his retirement from Grand Prix racing after a spectacular accident in France?

8 At which race did the ATS and Scirocco-Powell teams debut?

PIT STOP (3):

TEAM TALK: FERRARI

1 Which driver left Ferrari at the end of 1959 to join the Yeoman Credit team?

▼

2 Which Ferrari ended its racing life with a win in front of the impassioned Italian fans?

3 Some senior management personnel left Ferrari in 1961 after a dispute. Which team did they create?

4 At which race did the John Surtees/Ferrari partnership score its first victory?

5 At the last two races of the 1964 Ferraris appeared in unfamiliar guise. How?

6 In which year was Ferrari's Fiorano test track opened?

7 Which sportscar World Champion made his F1 debut for Ferrari in the 1968 Italian GP?

8 The 1975 Ferrari was designated 312-T. What did the T mean?

PIT STOP (4):

ENGINES

1 Which Japanese engine joined Honda for the 1989 season?

2 If Murray Walker said 'Senna's EF15 engine is working well' to which manufacturer would he be referring?

3 When did the first turbo engine race?

4 In 1975 there were only two makes of engine on the grid. Which?

5 When John Surtees won the 1964 World Championship did he use a V6, V8 or V12 engine?

6 In which race did the Honda air-cooled V8 make its one and only appearance?

▼

7 In 1986 Williams used a new Honda F engine. What did F signify?

8 Which engine won its first race at the Oesterreichring in 1970 and its last at Watkins Glen in 1979?

RESULTS

FIRST QUALIFYING

1 Michele Alboreto.
2 True.
3 Ivan Capelli.
4 Eddie Cheever who has had nine teams.
5 Nigel Mansell. He came third in the 1981 Belgian GP. Later that year John Watson had first and second.
6 Stefano Modena.
7 Adrian Campos.
8 Riccardo Patrese, who was acquitted.
9 Brabham.
10 Two — McLaren and Renault.
11 All have won a record seven races in one season.
12 Aguri Suzuki.
13 They are two of only four drivers to have driven 100 races or more without a win.
14 Alain Prost won the 1983 French GP in a Renault.
15 France.
16 False. Peter Gethin's 1971 Italian GP average was 150.75 mph. Still a record.

SECOND QUALIFYING

1 True. They were the USA West, USA East and the USA GP.
2 Monaco and Detroit.
3 True. To be exact it was six-tenths.
4 John Watson.
5 False. He did in 1981 and 1983, but Nigel Mansell's accident in Japan saved him the bother in 1987.
6 Keke Rosberg and Alan Jones.
7 True. Emmerson Fittipaldi won in 1973.
8 True. Jim Clark's oil pipe split and John Surtees' second place were enough for Surtees to win.
9 Argentina.
10 BMW.
11 Hungary.
12 He had chicken pox.
13 Nelson Piquet.
14 Monza. Eddie Cheever was third with Derek Warwick fourth in his slipstream.
15 Jack Brabham in 1966.
16 Gerard Ducarouge.

RACE TWO

1 Jo Siffert.
2 All 15 of the Starters finished and none had a pit stop.
3 Monaco, Australia, San Marino and Hungary.
4 The 1958 Moroccan GP.
5 He flew to Silverstone in a private plane!!
6 Didier Pironi.
7 1983.
8 Mike Hawthorn.
9 Stirling Moss and Tony Brooks.
10 Mercedes.
11 Vanwall.
12 Peter Collins.
13 Spanish GP.
14 Phillipe Etancelin.
15 1982.
16 Six.

PIT STOP (1):

SAN MARINO

1 1980.
2 Dino Ferrari, son of the late Enzo.
3 Villeneuve.
4 March.
5 Didier Pironi (1982) and Patrick Tambay (1983).
6 Because of a FOCA/FISA dispute only 14 cars took the start, and only five finished the race.
7 John Watson, fifth in 1983 for McLaren.
8 Elio de Angelis, Lotus.

PIT STOP (2):

A YEAR IN F1 1963

1 He won with maximum possible points; at that time his seven wins represented a record for one season.
2 Chris Amon.
3 It made him the first man to win World Championship races on two and four wheels.
4 Graham Hill (BRM).
5 The red flag was waved in mistake, leading some drivers to believe the start was delayed.
6 De Tomaso.
7 Ludovico Scarfiotti.
8 Belgian GP.

PIT STOP (3):

TEAM TALK: FERRARI

1 Tony Brooks, to be nearer his garage business in Weybridge.
2 The 246, at the 1960 Italian GP — the last before the introduction of new 1.5-litre regulations.
3 ATS.
4 German GP, 1963.
5 Following a row with the Italian Automobile the cars appeared in the blue and white of the North American Racing Team at Watkins Glen and Mexico.
6 1972.
7 Derek Bell.
8 Transversale — to signify the transverse-mounted gearbox.

PIT STOP (4):

ENGINES

1 Yamaha, with Zakspeed.
2 Renault in the 1986 Lotus.
3 British GP 1977 (Renault).
4 Ferrari and Ford-Cosworth.
5 V8.
6 French GP 1968; John Surtees was second but Jo Schlesser crashed and suffered fatal burns.
7 Frugal.
8 Ferrari's 3-litre flat 12.

SCORE		
1st QUAL.		
2nd QUAL.		
RACE		
PITSTOP (1)		
PITSTOP (2)		
PITSTOP (3)		
PITSTOP (4)		
TOTAL		

MONACO

FIRST QUALIFYING

1 Which team has had Renault, Honda and now Judd engines in the last three seasons?

2 Which was the chassis number of the all conquering McLaren in 1988?

3 Why was Ayrton Senna 'Blackflagged' in Brazil in 1988?

4 True or false? In the last ten years the winner of the Monaco GP has always been from the front row of the grid.

5 Stirling Moss, Niki Lauda and Ayrton Senna share what record?

6 Which driver had three extraordinary spectacular crashes at successive GPs in 1988?

7 How many times did the lead change hands at the 1953 Italian GP? Less than 10, between 10 and 20, 20 or more times?

8 Who got to No. 1 in the 'Motown' charts in 1988?

9 How many consecutive years have Honda powered the winning constructors team?

10 Which tyre manufacturer celebrated their first win in Brazil in 1978?

11 What did Alain Prost do at the 1988 French GP which he hadn't done for over two years?

12 Estoril and Spa in 1985 and ▶ Silverstone and Hockenheim in 1988 were all won by Ayrton Senna. What else did all these races have in common?

13 In which 1988 race did Alain Prost pass Niki Lauda's record number of points?

14 What did Satoru Nakajima manage at the 1988 Belgian GP for the first time?

15 How many 'Turbo' World Championships have there been?

16 True or false? When Brabham won the 1985 French GP on Pirelli tyres it was the first win on those tyres for 28 years. ▼

SECOND QUALIFYING

1 True or false? The most successful tyres in F1 have been Dunlop?

2 True or false? No engine has ever been as successful as the 1988 Honda.

3 Which World Champion won the 1970 Spanish GP then had a lean two years before winning there again?

4 Who won the 1972 South African GP — first of the season — and then didn't even qualify at Monaco?

5 Who is 'The Professor'?

6 How many times did Honda engines come 1-2-3 in 1988? Two times, four times or six times?

7 Although he didn't win the title in 1988, Alain Prost actually scored more points than any driver has ever scored before. True or false?

8 Alain Prost came first or second at every 1988 Grand Prix bar two. Which?

9 What was significant about the Renault RSO I?

10 Which was the only race of 1988 without a McLaren on pole?

▲

11 How many wins did Michele Alboreto's five years at Ferrari yield?

12 True or false? The McLaren-Honda retired with mechanical failure only once throughout 1988.

13 Which team won most pole positions in 1986?

14 How long is it since Brabham have won the constructors' title?

15 Which ex-World Champion was team leader of the ill-starred Team Haas?

16 Which was the only 1986 GP where Williams did not score a point?

RACE DAY

1 Which was the one race Alfa Romeo drivers did not win in 1950?

2 True or false? In 1952 Ferrari drivers occupied the top four Championship places.

3 The 1953 Italian GP saw Ferrari at last beaten, by a team gaining its first win. Who?

4 How many times did the Coventry-Climax Lotus win in the 47-race history of the 1½ litre Formula?

▼

6 Who was at the wheel when BRM first scored a GP victory?

7 Which car claimed its first GP victory in 1958?

8 What was so revolutionary about Colin Chapman's Lotus 25?

9 Which team totally dominated the 1955 season?

10 Who returned to drive for Maserati in 1956?

11 Which team won the 1962 constructors' title after 12 years of trying?

5 In 1952/3 the Ferrari Tipo 500 won every single round of the Championship. True or false?

12 Which car dominated the 1959 and 1960 seasons?

▲

13 In which year did Jack Brabham receive his knighthcod?

14 In which year did Maserati finally see a World Champion in one of their cars?

15 How many starts were there for the 1987 Austrian GP?

16 How many races did Vanwall win in 1958? Was it four, five or six?

PIT STOP (1):

MONACO

1 Which former World Champion was nicknamed 'Mr Monaco'?

2 What, on the technical side, made Ayrton Senna's 1987 win at Monaco so interesting?

▼

3 Lotus hold the record for Monaco wins. How many?

4 Which driver's first Grand Prix win was delayed by a controversial decision at Monaco in 1984?

5 Stirling Moss won Monaco three times, with two different cars. Which?

6 Which two drivers were involved in a spectacular accident at the Mirabeau corner in the 1986 Monaco GP?

7 In 1955 a car and driver went into the harbour at Monaco, the driver emerging relatively unscathed. Who was he and what car was he in?

8 'Tabac', 'Piscine' and 'La Rascasse' are all famous Monaco landmarks — but what are they?

PIT STOP (2):

A YEAR IN FORMULA ONE: 1974

1 How many drivers won races in the 15-round series: 5/7/9?

2 Who won the opening race and finished sixth five times?

3 What put the Grand Prix season in jeopardy?

4 Where did Ronnie Peterson score a resounding win on a circuit being used for the first time?

▼

5 Two new American teams came along. Name them.

6 If Murray said Graham Hill had just gone by in the T370 what car would you have seen?

7 A Japanese team made a brief appearance in Formula One. Name it.

8 Which now-familiar part of Grand Prix racing was introduced?

PIT STOP (3):

TRACK RECORD

1 Identify this World Championship circuit?

2 Who was the first winner of a World Championship race on this circuit?

3 No Briton has ever won there: true or false?

4 In which year in the 'eighties was there NOT a race there?

5 Who won the 1988 race there?

6 By the end of 1988 Alain Prost had yet to win there. True or false?

7 Who was the first polesitter there?

8 Which current driver finished in the points at the first World Championship race there?

9 Only two drivers have won twice there. Who?

10 Who was the first 'atmospheric' driver home in 1988?

PIT STOP (4):

SPONSORSHIP

1 Which was the first major sponsorship of the modern era?

2 At which race did Lotus cars first wear those colours?

3 Who were the principal sponsors of Lotus in 1980?

4 Parmalat had a long association with Brabham. Who or what was Parmalat?

5 Name at least three cigarette brands to figure on Grand Prix cars in 1988?

6 Which sponsor's non-tobacco product caused cancellation of BBC Grand Prix coverage?

7 Who were the first major sponsors of Williams?

8 With which team did Benetton enter Formula One?

RESULTS

FIRST QUALIFYING

1. Lotus.
2. —MP4/4.
3. He started illegally in the spare car.
4. False. On seven occasions he was, but three times he wasn't.
5. Successive pole positions. (Six.)
6. Philippe Alliot at Monaco and Mexico.
7. The lead changed 22 times.
8. Ayrton Senna, who won the Detroit GP.
9. Three.
10. Michelin.
11. Grabbed Pole Position.
12. Wet races.
13. Monaco.
14. Outqualified team-mate Nelson Piquet.
15. Four. Prost, Senna, Piquet and Lauda.
16. True. Their last success had been in 1957.

SECOND QUALIFYING

1. False. Goodyear have won nearly three times more races.
2. False. Honda won 15 races in 1988 and a Ford powered all 15 winners in 1973 as well.
3. Jackie Stewart.
4. Mario Andretti.
5. Alain Prost.
6. Two times. San Marino and Adelaide.
7. True. But because of the best 11 rule he had to drop some.
8. British (Silverstone) and Italian (Monza).
9. First turbo car.
10. British GP.
11. Three.
12. True.
13. Lotus. Eight times.
14. 21 years.
15. Alan Jones.
16. Austria.

RACE THREE

1. Indianapolis — which formed part of the championship until 1960.
2. True.
3. Maserati.
4. Twenty-two times.
5. False. It did not win Indianapolis nor the 1953 Italian GP.
6. Jo Bonnier.
7. Cooper.
8. It was a monocoque frame.
9. 1955.
10. Stirling Moss.
11. BRM.
12. Cooper.
13. 1979.
14. 1957, when Fangio took the title.
15. Three.
16. Six.

PIT STOP (1):

MONACO

1. Graham Hill, winner of the race five times.
2. His Lotus was the first car to win a Grand Prix with an 'active' suspension system.
3. Nine.
4. Ayrton Senna's: his Toleman was catching Alain Prost's McLaren when the race was stopped because of torrential rain.
5. Maserati (1956) and Lotus (1960 and 1961).
6. The Lola of Patrick Tambay catapulted off the Tyrrell of Martin Brundle, but both drivers escaped unhurt.
7. Alberto Ascari in a Lancia. Having survived that, he was killed shortly afterwards in sportscar testing.
8. The tobacconist's shop, swimming pool and a restaurant.

PIT STOP (2):

A YEAR IN F1 1974

1. Seven.
2. Denny Hulme (McLaren).
3. The oil crisis.
4. Dijon-Prenois.
5. Penske and Parnelli.
6. A Lola.
7. MAKI.
8. Qualifying practice.

PIT STOP (3):

TRACK RECORD

1. Montreal.
2. Gilles Villeneuve, 1978.
3. False. Nigel Mansell won for Williams in 1986.
4. 1987.
5. Ayrton Senna, McLaren.
6. True: at that stage Prost had never won in North America.
7. Jean-Pierre Jarier, Lotus.
8. Riccardo Patrese.
9. Alan Jones (1979-80), Nelson Piquet (1982, 1984).
10. Thierry Boutsen (Benetton) in fourth place.

PIT STOP (4):

SPONSORSHIP

1. Gold Leaf Team Lotus, 1968.
2. Spanish GP.
3. Essex.
4. An Italian dairy products firm.
5. Camel, Marlboro, West, Gitanes, Barclay.
6. Durex, on the Surtees car.
7. Saudia, 1978: they stayed till 1984.
8. Tyrrell in 1983.

SCORE		
1st QUAL.		
2nd QUAL.		
RACE		
PITSTOP (1)		
PITSTOP (2)		
PITSTOP (3)		
PITSTOP (4)		
TOTAL		

MEXICO

FIRST QUALIFYING

1 What was the first Grand Prix to be held behind the Iron Curtain?

2 Which driver had the misfortune to twice break both ankles?

3 Why were the drivers in a state of revolt before the 1987 Brazilian GP?

4 Why was Alain Prost denied his 1985 San Marino victory?

5 Who caused Ligier's absence at the start of the 1987 season?

6 Who crashed dramatically at 200 mph at San Marino in 1987 and as a result was considered medically unfit to race?

7 True or false? The 4.3 mile long Spa-Francorchamps circuit is composed entirely of public roads?

8 Why did Ivan Capelli appear in Brazil in 1987 in a F3000 car for an F1 race?

9 Who stepped into the breach to save Ligier when Alfa withdrew their engines?

10 Where was the first ever pole position for an 'active suspension' car?

11 Which two drivers tangled in Australia 1985, Brazil 1986 and Belgium 1987?

12 Who is the only man to suffer an 'Instant' disqualification in GP history?

13 Who won the last three Detroit GPs in a row?

14 Who managed to win the 1986 British GP — even though he was stuck on the grid?

15 Who at the 1987 British GP re-fuelled on the circuit (illegal) was push started (also illegal) and ignored the end of practice chequered flag (even more illegal)?

16 Which engine enjoyed a 1-2-3-4 at Silverstone in 1987?

SECOND QUALIFYING

1 Where did the 1987 World Champion win his first GP of that year?

2 What car was on the front row of the grid at Hungary in 1987 for the first time since Germany 1985?

3 Who had the misfortune to hit a deer that had strayed on to the course in Austria?

4 What did Ferrari manage to do in Portugal in 1987 for the first time in 2½ years?

5 Who was fined for hitting an official in Mexico in 1987?

▲

6 What does the superstitious Stefano Modena do with his glove?

7 How many drivers contested the 1988 championship?

8 Apart from the races he missed through injury, how many races in succession saw Nigel Mansell on the front row of the grid during seasons 1987/8?

9 How many different teams occupied the top eight places in Mexico in 1988. Four, six or eight?

10 In which 1988 race did Minardi achieve their first point in 52 races?

▼

11 Jonathan Palmer is a qualified doctor. But which qualified dentist drove for Ferrari?

12 Which country was the most represented in the 1989 season?

13 Who was the only Swiss driver of the 1989 season?

14 True or false? The maximum distance for a GP is now 305 km.

15 Why did Yannick Dalmas not appear in Australia in 1988?

16 Which engines appeared on the grid in 1989 for the first time ever?

RACE DAY

1 The Arrows team have been waiting for a win for ten years. Who came closest for them?

2 Which former World Champion was killed in a road accident in 1966?

3 Whose death, while testing at Monza 1955, caused Lancia to withdraw from racing?

4 True or false? Stirling Moss won the inaugural race at SIX circuits.

▼

5 How many wins separate Ayrton Senna's first victory in 1985 and his last to the end of 1989?

6 What have Derek Warwick, Eddie Cheever, Andrea De Cesaris and Jean-Pierre Jarier in common?

7 Who brought Michelin their first World Championship?

8 Which great champion made his debut in the 1960 Belgian GP?

9 Which was the last front-engined car to take part in a GP?

10 With the exception of the Italian GP, which was boycotted, which engine won every round of the 1960 championship?

11 What was unusual about the Ferguson P99 which ran at Aintree in 1961?

12 What, now demolished, gave its name to the Mirabeau corner at Monaco?

13 Who did Colin Chapman sack to make way for Jim Clark?

14 Who was the first woman driver to race in F1?

15 Who had 'Jesus Saves' emblazoned on his car?

16 Two fathers and sons have raced in F1: name them.

PIT STOP (1):

THE HOST COUNTRY

1 What is the name of the Mexico circuit, and why?

2 The Mexican GP returned to the World Championship calendar in 1986. When was the last Championship race there before that date?
▼

3 Who won that race, and what was unfortunate about its closing stages?

4 How many Mexican Grands Prix were there up to and including that 1970 race?

5 In 1988 one driver was extremely lucky to walk away from a major accident in qualifying — and had his car rebuilt in time for the race. Who, what team?

6 Two Americans have won the Mexican GP. Who, and in which years?

7 The revival of the Mexican GP in 1986 saw first victories for which driver and team?

8 Which Frenchman made his GP debut in Mexico in 1987?

PIT STOP (2):

A YEAR IN FORMULA ONE: 1980

1 Who won his first race at Long Beach and went on to be runner-up for the Drivers' Title?

2 Which circuit, now a regular, held its first GP in 1980?

3 Which team, still racing now, debuted in South Africa with Eddie Cheever driving?

4 Which two former World Champions retired at the end of the 1980 season?

5 Why were the Arrows team never short of attractive women?

6 Who made a mistake on the first corner at Watkins Glen, dropped to 12th and then blasted through to win?
▼

7 Who were Nelson Piquet's two team-mates at Brabham?

8 Which lady failed to qualify her Williams at the British GP?

PIT STOP (3):

TEAM TALK: McLAREN

1 Who replaced Bruce McLaren for a few races after the team founder's untimely death?
▼

2 In which race did a McLaren score its first World Championship points?

3 McLaren's best performance in 1971 was with a Roger Penske-entered car in the Canadian GP. Result and driver, please?

4 Why were McLaren sweet-smelling in 1972?

5 In 1972 McLaren had three contracted drivers. Who?

6 What engine powered the McLaren M54 whose début was at the 1972 Canadian GP?

7 Who drove the experimental 4WD McLaren on its only race outing in 1969?

8 Nowadays we are used to McLaren domination. When did they FIRST win a Championship?

PIT STOP (4):

PICTURE THIS

1 Where did this take place?
▼

PHOTO: ALLSPORT

2 Which two drivers were involved?

3 In what year was the incident?

4 For one of the drivers this coming-together was particularly significant. Which one and why?

5 Who won the race in question?

6 Arguably this accident 'gave' the Constructors' Championship to which team?

7 One driver in the race was blackflagged. Who?

8 In what year was the last Grand Prix held at this circuit?

RESULTS

FIRST QUALIFYING

1 Hungarian GP 1986.
2 Marc Surer.
3 Because FISA introduced a scale of fees for the Super Licence.
4 Because it was found his car was 2 kilos underweight.
5 Rene Arnoux. He ridiculed the Alfa-Romeo engine and the Italians withdrew support for the team in a huff. Despite the FISA ruling that teams must appear at all races this was considered a special case.
6 Nelson Piquet.
7 True.
8 The new March car was not ready to race. But FISA insist manufacturers enter every race. So March used their old F3000 car.
9 Megatron.
10 San Marino 1987.
11 Ayrton Senna and Nigel Mansell.
12 Christian Danner, after a coming together with Michele Alboreto in Monaco 1987.
13 Ayrton Senna.
14 Nigel Mansell. His drive shaft broke at the start, but an accident meant restarting the race.
15 Piercarlo Ghinzani.
16 Honda.

SECOND QUALIFYING

1 Germany.
2 A Ferrari (Gerhard Berger).
3 Stefan Johansson driving a McLaren in 1987.
4 Get Pole Position.
5 Ayrton Senna, who lost his temper with the poor man after he refused a push start.
6 Wears it inside out.
7 35.
8 16.
9 Four. McLaren were one and two, Ferrari were three and four, Arrows were five and six, and Benetton seven and eight.
10 USA East.
11 Tony Brooks.
12 Italy, with 14 drivers.
13 Gregor Foitek.
14 True. It was reduced from 320 km in 1989.
15 He had Legionnaire's Disease.
16 Lamborghini and Yamaha.

RACE FOUR

1 True. He won the first races held at Ain Diab, Aintree, Monsanto, Oporto, Pescara and Riverside.
2 Guiseppe Farina.
3 Alberto Ascari.
4 Thierry Boutsen grabbed second place at the 1985 San Marino GP.
5 20.
6 They have all failed to win a GP in 100 or more attempts.
7 Jody Scheckter.
8 Jim Clark.
9 The Scarab. Built and financed by an American group.
10 Coventry Climax.
11 It was four wheel drive.
12 Mirabeau Hotel.
13 Innes Ireland.
14 Maria Therese De-Fillipis.
15 Alex Ribero.
16 Tim Parnell and his father Reg. Hans Stuck and his father H. J. Stuck.

PIT STOP (1):

MEXICO

1 Autodromo Hermanos Rodriguez, after Mexican brothers Pedro and Riccardo, killed in racing cars.
2 1970.
3 Jacky Icxk in a Ferrari. Spectators surged on to the circuit as soon as he had won, the lack of crowd control contributing to the temporary demise of Mexico as a World Championship venue.
4 Eight.
5 Philippe Alliot, Larrousse Calmels Lola.
6 Dan Gurney (Brabham, 1964) and Richie Ginther (1965, Honda).
7 Gerhard Berger, Benetton.
8 Yannick Dalmas, Lola: he was classified ninth.

PIT STOP (2):

A YEAR IN F1 1980

1 Nelson Piquet.
2 Imola, which held the Italian GP the one year Monza didn't. Now holds San Marino.
3 Osella.
4 Jody Scheckter and Emmerson Fittipaldi.
5 They were sponsored by Penthouse magazine.
6 Alan Jones.
7 Hector Rebaque and Ricardo Zunino.
8 Desire Wilson.

PIT STOP (3):

TEAM TALK: McLAREN

1 Dan Gurney.
2 Monaco 1967: Bruce McLaren was fourth in a McLaren BRM.
3 Third: Mark Donohue.
4 They were sponsored by Yardley.
5 Denny Hulme, Peter Revson, Brian Redman.
6 BMW U-12.
7 Derek Bell, British GP.
8 1974: both constructors' and (Fittipaldi) drivers' titles.

PIT STOP (4):

PICTURE THIS

1 Zandvoort.
2 Nelson Piquet and Alain Prost.
3 1983.
4 Alain Prost — he lost the Championship to Piquet by just two points.
5 René Arnoux.
6 Ferrari.
7 Manfred Winkelhock.
8 1985.

SCORE		
1st QUAL.		
2nd QUAL.		
RACE		
PITSTOP (1)		
PITSTOP (2)		
PITSTOP (3)		
PITSTOP (4)		
TOTAL		

USA

ONE WAY
GOODYEAR
ICEBERG
ICEBERG
ONE WAY
FOSTERS
ICEBERG
CAMEL
CAMEL

FIRST QUALIFYING

1 Name three drivers who drove for more than one team in 1989.

2 At which race did Alain Prost set an all-time record with his 28th victory?

3 Who is the only winner to date of the Jim Clark Trophy?

4 Which driver's autobiography is entitled *To Hell and Back*?

5 Which driver was dismissed in acrimonious circumstances after just one race for Ferrari in 1985?

6 In which car did Niki Lauda, James Hunt and Ronnie Peterson all make their debuts?

7 During 1988, which team ran cars with fuel cells divided into two?

8 Andrea De Cesaris is one of the most experienced drivers of Formula One, but when did he make his debut: 1979? 1980? 1982?

▼

9 Ron Dennis leads McLaren, the most successful team in recent history. When did he first enjoy that position?

10 Who made his debut in the final race of the 1987 season in Adelaide?

11 In 1989 Formula One was fully atmospheric again. When was the last non-turbo victory?

12 What was the one race McLaren failed to win in 1988?

13 Between 1973 and 1985 which circuit shared with Paul Ricard the honour of staging the French GP?

14 If you were at the Bus Stop which GP would go by?

15 Only two Grands Prix have been ever-present on the calendar. Which?

16 What was the former name of Benetton Formula?

▼

SECOND QUALIFYING

1 Who was the first Belgian to win a World Championship race?

2 Which season brought Graham HIl the first of his two world titles?

6 When did Zakspeed enter Formula One?

7 Which circuit — Silverstone, Monaco, Monza — staged the first World Championship GP?

11 Which driver fell off a boat and broke a rib before the 1989 season?

12 Who was the last British World Champion?

13 Benetton had won only one GP to the end of 1988. Which?

3 In which two seasons did the great Colin Chapman/Jim Clark reign supreme?

4 Which American race counted towards the Drivers' Championship until 1960?

5 Which famous team has a Prancing Horse as its emblem?

8 Which country's GP has visited most different venues?

9 Which GP qualifier is a qualified GP?

10 When was the Constructors' World Championship inaugurated: 1954/1958/1961?

▲

14 Which driver wore a black helmet with white stripes?

15 'Clay' Regazzoni was a popular driver of the seventies. Real name and nationality?

16 What do the initials GPDA stand for?

RACE DAY

▲

1 In 1984 Niki Lauda beat Alain Prost to the title by half a point. At which race?

2 Where and when was the first Japanese GP held?

3 If you were in the City of Churches which GP would you be attending?

4 Gerhard Berger made his debut in the 1984 Austrian GP. In which car?

5 Which driver lost his life during practice for the 1973 US GP?

6 In which race did Yannick Dalmas make his debut?

7 Which was the second team to develop an 'active hydraulic suspension' car?

8 Who was the first driver to win the Championship in a British car?

9 Who holds the unusual distinction of having started from pole position in his first and last Grands Prix?

10 What do Jackie Stewart, Niki Lauda, Nelson Piquet and Alain Prost have in common?

11 Where did the 3-litre Ford-Cosworth DFV V8 engine start its series of 155 wins?
▼

12 What does FOCA stand for?

13 In 1988, what was the MINIMUM weight of a turbocharged Grand Prix car?

14 Who was the first driver to score World Championship points in a car of his own manufacture?

15 Which car, in 1988, was known as 'the blue Ferrari'?

16 How many nations have had a World Champion? (NB: Scotland and England treated as separate nations!) 8, 10, 12?

PIT STOP (1):

USA

1 Name at least four circuits on which World Championship Grands Prix have been run in the United States.

2 Sebring staged the US GP only once. When, and who won?

3 That Sebring race saw a famous driver exert himself more than usual. How, and with what result?

4 Who was disqualified after taking a brilliant second place in Detroit in 1984?

5 No American driver has ever won the US GP. True or false?

6 What was significant about Michele Alboreto's victory for Tyrrell at Detroit in 1983?

7 How many times has Alain Prost won the US GP?

8 Who was the last Grand Prix winner at Watkins Glen?
▼

PIT STOP (2):

A YEAR IN FORMULA ONE: 1954

1 In 1954 Juan Manuel Fangio won the Argentine GP — at the wheel of which car?

2 Mercedes rewrote the limits of Formula One technology with their new car. What was its designation?
▼

3 Who brought the Mercedes winning streak to a temporary halt?

4 Which long-awaited car made its debut in the final race of the season?

5 Who were the drivers of the two Mercedes that took a stunning 1-2 result in the team's first GP?

6 Who was leading driver for France's Gordini team?

7 Which was the closing race of the season?

8 For which team was Stirling Mcss driving in 1954?

PIT STOP (3):

TEAM TALK: WILLIAMS

1 In 1989, for the first time in a decade, Williams did not enjoy Mobil sponsorship. Why?

2 What was the designation of P. Head's first Williams design?

3 What was the first race at which Williams used Honda engines?

4 Who was FW's driver when he entered a March in 1971?

5 What landmark was Williams first to achieve in the Constructors' Championship?

6 How many different drivers occupied a Williams cockpit in 1975?

7 Who led the Williams team in 1975?

8 Where was Williams' first GP win with the hydraulic suspension car?

PIT STOP (4):

THE WORLD CHAMPIONS (2)

1 Name the 1961 World Champion.

2 Which World Champion was called 'Il grande John' by his team's passionate followers?

3 Keke Rosberg had just one win in his title year. Where?

4 Who was the first Brazilian to take the title?

5 Two drivers share the lowest number of career wins by a World Champion — and they have the same initial. Who?

6 How many Italian World Champions have there been?

7 No German has ever been World Champion. True or false?

8 Denny Hulme had his first victory in the same year that saw him become champion. Where, what year?

RESULTS

FIRST QUALIFYING

1 Alboreto, Herbert, Dalmas, Raphanel, and Gachot.
2 Portuguese GP 1987.
3 Jonathan Palmer (Tyrrell 1987).
4 Niki Lauda's.
5 Rene Arnoux.
6 March.
7 Ligier.
8 1980 — Alfa Romeo.
9 1981.
10 Stefano Modena (Brabham).
11 Detroit 1983 — Michele Alboreto in a Tyrrell.
12 Italian GP, won by Gerhard Berger (Ferrari).
13 Dijon-Prensis.
14 Belgian — it's at Spa-Francorchamps.
15 British and Italian.
16 Toleman Motorsport.

SECOND QUALIFYING

1 Jacky Ickx — French GP 1968.
2 1962.
3 1963 and 1965.
4 Indianapolis 500.
5 Ferrari.
6 1985.
7 Silverstone 1950.
8 US — 8.
9 Jonathan Palmer.
10 1958.
11 Nelson Piquet.
12 James Hunt in 1976.
13 Mexican GP 1986.
14 Graham Hill.
15 Gianclaudio; Swiss.
16 Grand Prix Drivers' Association.

RACE FIVE

1 Portuguese GP.
2 Fuji 1976.
3 Australian — Adelaide is known as the City of Churches.
4 ATS.
5 Francois Cevert (Tyrrell).
6 Mexican GP, 1987.
7 Williams.
8 Jack Brabham (Cooper 1959).
9 Mario Andretti (US GP 1968, Lotus, Italian GP 1982, Ferrari).
10 Triple World Champions.
11 Dutch GP 1967; Jim Clark drove.
12 Formula One Constructors' Asssociation.
13 540 kgs.
14 Jack Brabham: Fourth, US GP 1962.
15 Rial — designed by ex-Ferrari man Gustav Brunner.
16 Twelve.

PIT STOP (1):

USA

1 Sebring; Riverside; Watkins Glen; Long Beach; Las Vegas; Detroit; Dallas; Phoenix.
2 1959: Bruce McLaren (Cooper-Climax).
3 Jack Brabham pushed his Cooper-Climax the last half-mile to the finish to take fourth place and the World Championship.
4 Martin Brundle, for alleged irregularities in his Tyrrell's fuel.
5 False: Mario Andretti (Lotus) won at Long Beach in 1977.
6 It was the last victory for a normally-aspirated car before turbocharging was outlawed in 1989.
7 Once, Phoenix 1989.
8 Alan Jones: Williams, 1980.

PIT STOP (2):

A YEAR IN F1 1954

1 Maserati.
2 W196.
3 Froilan Gonzalez in a Ferrari at Silverstone.
4 Lancia D50.
5 Juan Manuel Fangio and Karl Kling.
6 Jean Behra.
7 Spanish GP at Pedralbes (Barcelona).
8 Maserati — third in Belgium was his best result.

PIT STOP (3):

TEAM TALK: WILLIAMS

1 Because of Renault's Elf association.
2 FW06.
3 South African GP of 1983.
4 Henri Pescarolo.
5 Past 100 pts (120 in 1980).
6 Six.
7 Jacques Laffite.
8 Monza 1987, N. Piquet.

PIT STOP (4):

THE WORLD CHAMPIONS (2)

1 Phil Hill (US), Ferrari.
2 John Surtees (Ferrari, 1964).
3 Swiss GP, Dijon.
4 Emerson Fittipaldi, 1972 (Lotus).
5 Mike Hawthorn and Phil Hill, three wins each.
6 Only two: Farina and Ascari
7 True.
8 Monaco, 1967.

SCORE		
1st QUAL.		
2nd QUAL.		
RACE		
PITSTOP (1)		
PITSTOP (2)		
PITSTOP (3)		
PITSTOP (4)		
TOTAL		

CANADA

FIRST QUALIFYING

1 Who was the Dallara team's driver in 1988?

2 Which three teams made their debuts in Brazil in 1988?

3 Which current driver has driven for Hesketh, Osella, Tyrrell, Ligier, Renault, Benetton, Lola and Arrows?

4 True or false? Alain Prost scored in both his first two Grand Prix races.

5 True or false? There has never been a South African World Champion?
▼

6 Renault returned to Formula One in 1989. Before then, how many pole positions had Renault-engined cars secured: 20/35/50?

7 Which World Champion won the fewest World Championship races in his career?

8 Before the green light system was introduced, which flag was used to start a Grand Prix?

9 At each Grand Prix, what role does Sid Watkins play?

10 Only two teams have managed to grab Pole Position more than 100 times. Which?

11 Which two Japanese drivers had races in 1988?
▼

12 Why do marshals wave a blue flag?

13 Which team has won more Grands Prix than any other?

14 Who was the driver to break up the Senna/Prost domination of Pole Positions in 1988?

15 Each decade has its dominant force. Which driver won most Grands Prix in the 'seventies — Lauda, Stewart or Fittipaldi?

16 Who holds the record for most wins in a season?

SECOND QUALIFYING

1 True or false? James Hunt has won more Grands Prix than Nigel Mansell.

2 Who was the last New Zealander to win a Grand Prix?

3 What was Nelson Piquet's best position in a 1988 Grand Prix: 2nd, 3rd or 4th?

4 Which team has won more Grands Prix in succession than any other?

5 Which of these three men won most Grands Prix: Keke Rosberg, Jacques Laffite or Rene Arnoux?

▼

6 Who was the last Swede to win a Grand Prix?

7 True or false? Nobody has ever taken the title averaging fewer than three points a race.

8 What is the most successful engine in the history of Grand Prix racing?

9 Three Grand Prix teams have amassed over 1,000 Championship points. Name two.

10 Which team has won the Constructors' title by the biggest margin?

11 Who won his first Grand Prix in 1959, in only his eighth race at the age of 22?

12 Which are the two circuits on which the South African Grand Prix has been held?

13 Carlos Menditeguy, Onofre Marimon, Robert Mieres: three drivers, one nationality — which?

14 Nigel Mansell never took pole for Lotus. True or false?

15 Where did Ayrton Senna claim his first pole position?

16 Who substituted for Yannick Dalmas in the final race of the 1988 season?

RACE DAY

▲

1 Which well known French star of the 'fifties had a distinctive black and white chequered helmet?

2 By the end of 1989 this French driver had five points finishes — but never higher than sixth. Who?

3 Which driver is nicknamed 'Dustin Hoffman'?

4 Who was the 29th driver to register World Championship points in 1989?

5 Who won the last race in Indianapolis when it was a World Championship event?

6 Among early British contenders were the HWM cars. What did the initials stand for?

7 Where would you have gone to see Tarzan in Formula One?

8 Only once did an Amon car start a World Championship race. Where and when?

9 The Coventry-built Ferguson project 99 started only one World Championship race. Where and when?

10 Which was Jean-Pierre Beltoise's only victory?

11 Rene Arnoux drove a Renault to victory in the French GP — in which year?

12 For which British team did Peter Arundell drive?

13 Where, when and for whom did Thierry Boutsen make his Grand Prix debut?

14 Which is the only pole position of Andrea De Cesaris' long career?

15 What do Derek Warwick and Ayrton Senna have in common?

16 Where and when did Stirling Moss make his World Championship debut?

PIT STOP (1):

CANADA

1 The first four Canadian Grands Prix were marked by 1-2 finishes. By which teams?

2 The three circuits on which the Canadian round has been run share the same initial. Name them.

3 Who won the inaugural race in Montreal?

4 In which season was Montreal excluded from the World Championship calendar?

5 The last driver to lose his life in a Formula One race was in Canada. Who, when?

6 Only one driver has won the Canadian GP twice in different cars. Can you name driver and vehicles?

▲

7 Which American driver had his final Grand Prix win in Canada in 1973?

8 Which car did Jody Scheckter drive to victory in Canada in 1977?

PIT STOP (2):

A YEAR IN FORMULA ONE: 1967

▲

1 Who drove to victory in the Italian Grand Prix?

2 Who won the first World Championship Canadian Grand Prix?

3 Who was called up to drive the second Ferrari at the Mexican Grand Prix?

4 1967 European Formula Two Champion, made his Formula One debut that year in Italy and finished sixth: who was he?

5 Which future World Champion had talks with Ferrari at the end of 1967 but never drove for them?

6 Where did Denny Hulme score his maiden victory?

7 Which three drivers formed Ferrari's line up at the start of the season?

8 Who won the Constructors' World Championship?

PIT STOP (3):

TRACK RECORD

▲

1 Name this much-loved circuit.

2 What is the name of the fearsome corner at the bottom of the hill after the hairpin?

3 And of the hairpin itself?

4 Who was the first World Championship racewinner there?

5 How many times did Jim Clark win there?

6 Which American car had its only GP win there?

7 Which Constructor also registered a maiden GP win there?

8 Gunnar Nilsson scored his sole GP victory there: true or false?

PIT STOP (4):

RULES AND REGULATIONS

▲

1 Which major rule change in 1958 concerned fuel?

2 Which change in race distance took place in 1958?

3 Which year saw the introduction of a 1.5 litre formula?

4 From 1961 to 1965 what was a Formula One car's minimum dry weight?

5 From January 1972 what was the maximum number of cylinders?

6 In 1961 the 1,500cc ruling went together with compulsory use of commercial fuel — and which other major rule change?

7 In which year did the 3-litre category come into force?

8 What was the distribution of points per race up to and including 1959?

RESULTS

FIRST QUALIFYING

1. Alex Caffi.
2. Rial, EuroBrun and Dallara.
3. Eddie Cheever.
4. True.
5. False. Jody Scheckter won in 1979.
6. 50 from 1979-86.
7. Mike Hawthorn and Phil Hill both won three — and all for Ferrari.
8. National flag of the host country.
9. Official medical supervisor.
10. Lotus and Ferrari.
11. Satoru Nakajima and Aguri Suzuki.
12. To show a driver he is about to be overtaken.
13. Ferrari (97 to end of 1989.
14. Gerhard Berger, who took Pole Position in the British Grand Prix in his Ferrari.
15. Lauda (17).
16. Ayrton Senna. His eight wins 1988 beat the seven held by Jim Clark and Alain Prost.

SECOND QUALIFYING

1. False. James Hunt won ten, but Nigel Mansell won 15 by end of 1989.
2. Denis Hulme, who won in Argentina in 1974 in a McLaren.
3. He was third three times.
4. Ferrari. In 1952/53 they won 14. In modern times McLaren's total of 11 in 1988 is the best.
5. Arnoux with seven leads Lafitte on six and Rosberg on five.
6. Ronnie Peterson, who won in Austria in 1978 for Lotus.
7. False. In 1982 Keke Rosberg (Williams) did it on 2.93.
8. Ford DFV with 155 wins.
9. Lotus, McLaren and Ferrari.
10. McLaren were 134 points clear of Ferrari in 1988 — easily a record.
11. Bruce McLaren.
12. East London and Kyalami.
13. Argentine.
14. False: his Lotus-Renault was on pole in Dallas in 1984.
15. Portugal, 1985.
16. Pierre-Henri Raphanel.

RACE SIX

1. Jean Behra.
2. Philippe Alliot.
3. Ivan Capelli.
4. Emanuele Pirro.
5. Jim Rathman.
6. Hersham and Walton Motors.
7. Holland — it's the hairpin at Zandvoort.
8. Spain 1974: Chris Amon himself had to retire.
9. British GP 1961: the four-wheel drive machine was driven by Fairman and Moss.
10. Monaco 1972; BRM.
11. 1982.
12. Lotus (1964-1966).
13. Belgium, Arrows, 1983.
14. USA West (Long Beach), 1982.
15. Each made his GP debut with Toleman.
16. Swiss GP 1951, Bremgarten, in an HWM.

PIT STOP (1):

CANADA

1. Brabham (1967 and 1969), McLaren (1968) and Ferrari (1970).
2. Mosport, Mont Tremblant and Montreal.
3. Gilles Villeneuve (Ferrari, 1980).
4. 1987.
5. Riccardo Paletti 1982.
6. Jacky Ickx: Brabham (1969) and Ferrari (1970).
7. Peter Revson (McLaren).
8. Wolf.

PIT STOP (2):

A YEAR IN F1 1967

1. John Surtees.
2. Jack Brabham.
3. Jonathan Williams.
4. Jacky Ickx.
5. Jackie Stewart.
6. Monaco.
7. Bandini, Scarfiotti and Amon.
8. Brabham.

PIT STOP (3):

TRACK RECORD

1. Spa-Francorchamps.
2. Eau Rouge.
3. La Source.
4. Juan Manuel Fangio in 1950.
5. 4: 1962-65.
6. Dan Gurney's Eagle Weslake in 1967.
7. McLaren in 1968.
8. False: he won the Belgian GP in 1977, but at Zolder.

PIT STOP (4):

RULES AND REGULATIONS

1. Alcohol-based fuels were replaced by pump petrol.
2. Shortened from 500 to 300 kilometres.
3. 1961.
4. 450 kilograms.
5. 12.
6. Cars had to have self-starters.
7. 1966.
8. 8-6-4-3-2, and 1 for fastest lap.

SCORE		
1st QUAL.		
2nd QUAL.		
RACE		
PITSTOP (1)		
PITSTOP (2)		
PITSTOP (3)		
PITSTOP (4)		
TOTAL		

FRANCE

BP
BP
RHÔNE-POULENC
Shell
SOCIETE
MARSEILLAISE
DE CREDIT
Philips Car Stereo
GOODYEAR
Shell
OPEL

FIRST QUALIFYING

1 Grand Prix debut 1968 at Watkins Glen . . . 12 victories . . . His teams included Lotus, Ferrari and Williams: who is he?

2 How many victories did John Watson score in Formula One? 2/5/7?

3 Which driver was sacked before the 1989 Portuguese GP?

4 Alain Prost was France's first World Champion: true or false?

5 Which are the only two Grands Prix to have figured in the World Championship every year?

6 How many races counted towards the inaugural World Championship: 7/10/12?

7 When did Ferrari first win a Grand Prix?

8 Name Ferrari's 1989 Team Manager?

9 Where did he score his first 'win' in that job?

10 What was the team now known as Rial first called?

11 Which is the quickest circuit in current World Championship use?

12 Two current drivers have scored over 400 World Championship points. Who?

13 Who, in 1989, said, 'motor racing is fun'?

14 What did Alain Prost do in 1989 that he had never done before?

15 Which current Grand Prix star relaxes by flying model aircraft?

16 Who drove when Penske achieved their lone World Championship victory?

SECOND QUALIFYING

▲

1 Who took over as manager of the Cooper team in 1963 after John Cooper's serious road accident?

2 Who is the youngest driver ever to win a World Championship race?

3 When was Formula One not Formula One?

4 What do the initials FISA stand for?

5 Who is its President?

6 Juan-Manuel Fangio was World Champion five times yet won just once in Britain. When?

7 What does the waving of a white flag denote?

8 Which World Champion was killed on the Guildford by-pass?

9 In 1972, which Grand Prix returned to the World Championship calendar after a 12-year absence?

10 What is the name of the small circuit at Le Mans that hosted the French Grand Prix in 1967 — and never again?

11 The Cavallino Rampante is a famous Formula One emblem. What is it, and whose?

12 Which famous former Lotus and Tyrrell designer died in 1989?

13 Which popular driver was known as Seppi?

14 In which year did he win the British GP?

15 How many pole positions did Niki Lauda occupy in his 1975 World title-winning year? 3/7/9?

16 Which infamous race had only seven cars running at the finish, ended 12 laps early, saw 16 drivers crash in rain — and produced official results three days later?

RACE DAY

1 Why was James Hunt disqualified from first place in the 1976 Spanish Grand Prix?

2 Which driver competed in his first Grand Prix at Rouen in 1968 at the ripe old age of 40?

3 Why did Jackie Stewart miss the 1972 Belgian Grand Prix?

4 Jody Scheckter clinched the title in a Ferrari at Monza in 1979, but another team dominated the front row of the grid. Which?

5 Which famous driver had a stained glass window depicting his own racing helmet in his home?

6 What was the last victory for a Matra-engined car?

7 At which race did Stirling Moss record his first win for Maserati?

8 In the turbo era, what was the purpose of an intercooler?

9 Who was the winner of the 1987 Japanese Grand Prix?

10 Why did Juan Manuel Fangio have problems seeing where he was going at Silverstone in 1954?

11 Dijon 1979 saw the first Renault victory in the French Grand Prix — but everyone was spellbound by the duel for second place. Which two drivers fought it out?

12 Who is the youngest ever English driver to win a Grand Prix?

13 Which driver set a lap record at Brands Hatch in 1980 that stood for five years?

14 Which current racer has written an autobiography entitled *Driven to Win*?

15 Where did Jackie Stewart score the final win of his career?

16 Which driver was known as ▶ 'Quick Vic'?

PIT STOP (1):

FRANCE

1 How do strong drink and the French Grand Prix go hand-in-hand?

2 One circuit in France has staged the French Grand Prix only once. Which, and when?

3 How many times did Renault win their home Grand Prix?

4 What was significant about Nelson Piquet's victory in France in 1975?

5 What was significant about the French Grand Prix at Rheims in 1953?

▼

6 Hawthorn won at Rheims again in 1958, but the race was marred by the death of one of his team-mates. Who, and which team?

7 Which driver won his only Grand Prix victory at the first attempt in France in 1961?

8 At which French circuit would you have found a bend called 'Nouveau Monde', or 'New World'?

PIT STOP (2):

A YEAR IN FORMULA ONE: 1975

1 Which Ferrari drivers occupied the front row in Spain but took each other off on the first corner?

2 In the same race, whose Hill-Cosworth led the race but suffered an aerofoil failure and crashed killing four spectators?

3 Who refused to take part in that race in protest over safety standards?

4 Who put the Shadow on pole position in its first appearance, in Argentina?

5 In which race did the now familiar electronic timing first appear?

6 Who was black-flagged at the US Grand Prix and withdrawn by his team in protest?

7 March won their second Grand Prix. Who was the driver, and where?

▼

8 Apart from their cars, what did Brabham's drivers have in common?

PIT STOP (3):

TEAM TALK: BENETTON

1. What is the name of Benetton's 1989 designer?

2. When did Benetton assume overall control of their own team?

3. Which was the first pole position for a fully-fledged Benetton?

4. Why was Benetton's Thierry Boutsen disqualified from third place in the 1988 Belgian Grand Prix?

5. What make of tyre helped Benetton to their first Grand Prix win in Mexico in 1986?

6. What engines did the team use before Benetton assumed control?

7. In the days when Benetton was Toleman, who left in acrimonious circumstances to join Lotus?

8. Who assumed responsibilities as Benetton team manager after Peter Collins's departure in 1989?

PIT STOP (4):

DESIGNS ON FORMULA ONE

1. Who was fired by Ferrari in 1973 but brought back after a disastrous season?

2. Who designed Jackie Stewart's 1971 title-winning Tyrrell?

3. Which designer has been at McLaren, Brabham and Lola?

4. Who designed the first Brabham Grand Prix car?

5. Who was behind Lancia's D50 Grand Prix car?

6. The Honda RA300 won 'out of the box' at Monza in 1967. Whose design?

7. In 1969 a Cosworth four-wheel-drive car appeared but did not race. Whose design?

8. The McLaren MP4/4 made history with 15 wins in 16 in 1988 races. Who was chiefly responsible for its design?

RESULTS

FIRST QUALIFYING

1 Mario Andretti.
2 Five.
3 Bertrand Gachot of Onyx.
4 True.
5 British and Italian.
6 Seven — including Indianapolis.
7 1951, GB — Froilan Gonzales.
8 Cesare Fiorio.
9 Italian GP 1970 (Ferrari).
10 ATS.
11 Silverstone.
12 Alain Prost and Nelson Piquet.
13 Ron Dennis.
14 Won the US GP (Phoenix).
15 Ayrton Senna.
16 John Watson (Austria 1976).

SECOND QUALIFYING

1 Ken Tyrrell.
2 Bruce McLaren: 22 when he won the 1959 US GP in a Cooper.
3 1952-53, when Formula two regulations were adopted.
4 Fédération Internationale du Sport Automobile.
5 Jean-Marie Balestre.
6 Presence of a slow-moving vehicle on the track.
7 1956 (Ferrari).
8 Mike Hawthorn.
9 Argentine GP — won that year by Jackie Stewart (Tyrrell).
10 Circuit Bugatti.
11 Prancing Horse — Ferrari's.
12 Maurice Phillippe.
13 Jo Siffert.
14 1968, in a Lotus 49 entered by Rob Walker.
15 Nine.
16 British GP 1975.

RACE SEVEN

1 Post-race scrutineering found his McLaren to be 1.8 centimetres too wide.
2 Jo Schlesser in a Honda.
3 He had a bleeding duodenal ulcer.
4 Renault: Jabouille and Arnoux.
5 Keke Rosberg in Cookham Dean.
6 Canada, 1981 (Lafitte in a Ligier.
7 Monaco 1956.
8 To cool the air/fuel mixture between the compressor discharge and the engine intake.
9 Gerhard Berger.
10 His Mercedes had all-enveloping bodywork and he kept clipping the barrels used to make out parts of the course.
11 Villeneuve (Ferrari) and Arnoux (Renault).
12 Mike Hawthorn at 24.
13 Didier Pironi in his Ligier.
14 Nigel Mansell.
15 Nurburgring 1973.
16 Englishman Vic Elford, who drove for Cooper, McLaren and BRM between 1968 and 1971.

PIT STOP (1):

FRANCE

1 Drinks magnate Paul Ricard financed the circuit on which the French race has recently been run.
2 Le Mans, 1967, when Brabham won.
3 Four: 1979-81-82-83.
4 It was the last to date for Brabham.
5 Mike Hawthorn's victory was the first by an Englishman in the World Championship.
6 Luigi Musso, Ferrari.
7 Giancarlo Baghetti (Ferrari).
8 Rouen.

PIT STOP (2):

A YEAR IN F1 1975

1 Niki Lauda and Clay Regazzoni.
2 Rolf Stommelin's.
3 Emerson Fittipaldi, the reigning World Champion.
4 Jean-Pierre Jarier.
5 Brazilian Grand Prix.
6 Clay Regazzoni.
7 Vittorio Brambilla, Austrian Grand Prix.
8 First name Carlos — Pace and Reutemann.

PIT STOP (3):

TEAM TALK: BENETTON

1 Rory Byrne.
2 1986.
3 Austria 1986: Teo Fabi.
4 Fuel irregularities.
5 Pirelli — and without a stop.
6 HART Turbo.
7 Ayrton Senna.
8 Gordon Message.

PIT STOP (4):

DESIGNS ON FORMULA ONE

1 Mauro Forghieri.
2 Derek Gardner.
3 Ralph Bellamy.
4 Ron Tauranac.
5 Vittorio Jano.
6 Eric Broadley's.
7 Robin Herd's.
8 Steve Nichols.

SCORE		
1st QUAL.		
2nd QUAL.		
RACE		
PITSTOP (1)		
PITSTOP (2)		
PITSTOP (3)		
PITSTOP (4)		
TOTAL		

BRITAIN

Shell Oils
Shell Oils
Shell Oils
Shell Oils
Shell Oils
Shell Oils

FIRST QUALIFYING

1 In which year did the Zakspeed team make its debut?

2 Nigel Mansell's victory in Brazil in 1989 was the first there by a Briton. True or false?

3 Whose helmet bore the colours of the London Rowing Club?

4 If you were on Ocean Boulevard which race would you have been watching?

5 In which two years did the great partnership of Jim Clark and Colin Chapman win the title?

6 Who is the only man to have won Formula One and Motor Cycling World Titles?

7 What is the name of the famous tight chicane at the San Marino circuit?

8 What race saw Nigel Mansell make his debut?

9 Who is the first and only Belgian to have won a GP?

10 Two 'new' trophies were awarded in 1987. One was the Jim Clark Trophy. What was the other?

11 There hasn't been an Italian World Champion since 1953. True or false?

12 How many pole positions has René Arnoux claimed in his long Formula One career: 6/12/18/24?

13 Only two teams have scored more than 120 points in a season. Which?

14 Which two Americans have been World Champions?

▼

15 Who was the last German to win a GP?

16 Which German was dropped by the AGS team halfway through the 1989 season?

SECOND QUALIFYING

1 The Nurburgring is the longest circuit ever used for a GP. True or False?

2 Which World Champion could have been an Olympic marksman?

3 In terms of mileage, which is the shortest circuit used for a GP?

4 True or False? There has never been a German World Champion.

5 Before Nannini in 1989, who was the last Italian to win a GP?

6 Which World Champion played at the Wimbledon Junior Tennis Championships?

7 Although held in the heart of Italy, the San Marino race has only ever once been won by an Italian. Who was he?

8 Why did Derek Warwick miss the 1989 French Grand Prix?

▼

9 Who deputised for him?

10 Whose career in Formula One has the longest span.

11 The Jaguar team have never raced in Formula One. True or false?

12 What colours did McLaren race in BEFORE the familiar Marlboro Red?

13 Apart from victory, what other significant target did Ayrton Senna achieve at the 1989 Spanish GP?

14 How many times have Britons won the Title: 5, 10 or 15?

15 Who drove for the tiny Coloni team in 1988?

16 True or false: The British GP has always been held in July?

RACE DAY

1 There has been only one World Championship race in which every starter finished. Which?

2 Who were the Three Fs?

3 Which four British drivers finished in the first seven at Rio in 1989?

4 Which driver is a model railway enthusiast?

5 Who drove the AGS in its first GP, in 1986?

6 René Arnoux is one of the most experienced drivers in the sport. When did he make his debut, and with which team?

7 What was the designation of the first Lotus GP car?

8 Where and when did the late Gunnar Nilsson claim his only Grand Prix victory?

9 Which French driver shared six 1-2 finishes with Jackie Stewart?

10 Which mid-fifties car was designated the W196?

11 Where did Alessandro Nannini score his first-ever points?

12 How many times did Keke Rosberg take pole position for McLaren? ▶

13 Which Frenchman was on pole at the 1984 French GP?

14 Who was the first Frenchman to score a World Championship point?

▼

15 Which famous French driver died in a powerboat accident?

16 How many French drivers scored points in 1988?

PIT STOP (1):

GREAT BRITAIN

1 Apart from Silverstone and Brands Hatch, which other track has been the venue for the British GP?

▼

2 Which driver's Grand Prix career was ended by an accident at the first corner of the 1986 British GP?

3 Williams' first Grand Prix win came at the British round. When, and through which driver?

4 Why was James Hunt disqualified after 'winning' the 1976 British Grand Prix?

5 Which driver handed over his car to Stirling Moss, thus sharing his victory in the 1957 British GP?

6 In 1977, an Englishman, an Irishman and a Welshman all took part in the British GP. Can you name them?

7 What landmark did Minardi achieve in the 1989 British GP?

8 What landmark did Keke Rosberg achieve during the British GP weekend of 1985?

PIT STOP (2):

A YEAR IN FORMULA ONE 1986

1 Derek Warwick returned to Formula One following the tragic loss of which popular driver?

2 Which two circuits figured in the Championship for the first time?

3 This was the year in which Keke Rosberg scored his last World Championship race victory: True or false?

4 It was the only year in Formula One to date for Johnny Dumfries. What was his best result?

▼

5 Where did Alain Prost win with nothing left?

6 Where on the Adelaide circuit did Nigel Mansell's famous blowout occur?

7 Where did a Minardi outqualify a Ferrari?

8 What was the type number of Gordon Murray's low-lying Brabham design?

PIT STOP (3):

TEAM TALK: MERCEDES

1 Who became J. M. Fangio's team-mate in 1955?

2 Name the great character who managed the team?

▼

3 How many GPs did Mercedes win in 1955?

4 What were Mercedes the first to use successfully in Formula One?

5 What make of tyre did Mercedes use for their entry into Formula One?

6 What was their popular nickname?

7 When did Mercedes withdraw from Formula One and why?

8 Who passed Fangio's Mercedes on the last corner of the last lap of the 1955 British GP?

PIT STOP (4):

ENGINES

1 Where and when did Lamborghini's V-12 score its first World Championship point?

2 Which engine powered Jim Clark to the 1965 world title?

3 At the end of which season did Coventry Climax withdraw from Formula One?

4 Who fielded the first gas turbine car in Grand Prix racing?

5 Whose engine made Jack Brabham World Champion in 1966?

6 Whose engines were in the 1966-67 works Coopers?

7 Which was the last GP win by an Alfa Romeo engine?

▼

8 Which was the only GP win for the Weslake engine?

RESULTS

FIRST QUALIFYING

1 1985.
2 True.
3 Graham Hill's.
4 The USA (West) GP at Long Beach, California.
5 1963 and 1965.
6 John Surtees.
7 Aqua Minerale.
8 Austria 1980 (Lotus).
9 Jackie Ickx and Thierry Boutsen.
10 The Colin Chapman Trophy — for the top 'atmospheric' team.
11 True.
12 Eighteen.
13 Williams and McLaren.
14 Phil Hill (1961) and Mario Andretti (1978).
15 Jochen Mass, Spain 1975 (McLaren).
16 Joachim Winkelhock.

SECOND QUALIFYING

1 False. The Pescara circuit used in 1957 was longer.
2 Jackie Stewart.
3 Monaco.
4 True.
5 Michele Alboreto, who won in Germany in 1985 for Ferrari.
6 James Hunt.
7 Elio De Angelis in 1985 (Lotus).
8 He was injured in a karting accident in Jersey.
9 Martin Donnelly.
10 Graham Hill: 16 years and 8 months.
11 True.
12 Orange.
13 His 40th pole position.
14 Ten.
15 Gabriele Tarquini.
16 False. In 1950 the first one was held in May.

RACE EIGHT

1 Holland 1961 — there were 15.
2 Giuseppe Farina, Luigi Fagioli, Juan Manuel Fangio (Alfa Romeo 1950).
3 Mansell/Warwick/Herbert/Palmer.
4 Riccardo Patrese.
5 Ivan Capelli at Monza.
6 1978, Martini.
7 Lotus 16 (1958).
8 Belgian GP at Zolder in 1977.
9 François Cévert.
10 Mercedes-Benz.
11 At Silverstone in 1988 with third place for Benetton.
12 Just once, at the 1986 German GP.
13 Patrick Tambay (Ferrari).
14 Maurice Trintignant in a Ferrari, Monaco 1955.
15 Didier Pironi.
16 Just one — no extra points for identifying Alain Prost.

PIT STOP (1):

GREAT BRITAIN

1 Aintree, five times between 1955 and 1962.
2 Jacques Laffite's.
3 1979, Clay Regazzoni.
4 For changing cars after the first-lap accident that stopped the original race.
5 Tony Brooks.
6 James Hunt, John Watson and Tom Pryce.
7 First time both drivers finished in the points — Martini fifth, Sala sixth.
8 The first-ever average speed for a Formula One lap of over 160 mph.

PIT STOP (2):

A YEAR IN F1 1986

1 Elio De Angelis, killed in testing in France.
2 Jerez, Spain and the Hungaroring near Budapest.
3 False: second at Monaco was his best result.
4 Fifth in Hungary.
5 At Imola — he coasted across the line out of fuel.
6 Brabham Straight.
7 Adelaide, where Andrea De Cesaris was 11th on the grid alongside Stefan Johansson.
8 BT55.

PIT STOP (3):

TEAM TALK: MERCEDES

1 Stirling Moss.
2 Alfred Neubauer.
3 Five.
4 Fuel injection.
5 Continental.
6 Silver Arrows.
7 1955, Le Mans disaster.
8 Stirling Moss — his Mercedes team-mate.

PIT STOP (4):

ENGINES

1 Spain 1989 — Philippe Alliot sixth in the Larrousse-Lola.
2 32-valve Coventry Climax V8.
3 1965.
4 Lotus, with the 1971 56B — which had 4WD to boot!
5 Repco's.
6 Maserati's.
7 Italian GP 1978 (Niki Lauda, Brabham).
8 Belgium 1967 in Dan Gurney's Eagle.

SCORE		
1st QUAL.		
2nd QUAL.		
RACE		
PITSTOP (1)		
PITSTOP (2)		
PITSTOP (3)		
PITSTOP (4)		
TOTAL		

GERMANY

FIRST QUALIFYING

1 In which year did Graham Hill win his *second* World Championship?

2 How much was Nigel Mansell fined after the 1989 Portuguese Grand Prix?

3 Which driver has won the World Championship by the narrowest margin?

4 How many 1-2 finishes did McLaren enjoy in 1988: 10/12/14?

5 Which driver quit Formula One in 1987 but returned as a World Champion?

6 With which team did Gerhard Berger make his debut in 1984?

7 True or false: no European ever won Indianapolis while that race was a World Championship event?

8 For which team did Elio De Angelis drive after Lotus? ▼

9 ▲ How long before the start of each Grand Prix is the pit lane closed?

10 Which famous English team boss died in December 1982?

11 Satoru Nakajima was the first Japanese driver to score a World Championship point: true or false?

12 How many different teams have had a World Champion? 12/14/16.

13 Who is the only driver to have put a Benetton on pole position?

14 Which well-known company is responsible for all Grand Prix timing?

15 Which is the only country currently allowed to stage two Grands Prix each year?

16 Who was the Earl of Dumfries' team-mate in 1986?

SECOND QUALIFYING

1 At which race in 1989 did Ayrton Senna claim his 41st pole position?

2 Which driver in 1980-81 scored points in 15 consecutive races?

3 What did Niki Lauda call his autobiography?

4 Which Frenchman — other than Alain Prost — scored points in his first Grand Prix — and in France?

5 What was Nigel Mansell's last pole position for Williams?

6 Whose surnames combined to give the name of the all-conquering Cosworth engine?

7 Where did Danny Sullivan score the only points of his one-year Grand Prix career?
▼

8 Which team in 1989 fielded a car designated JH24?

9 Which French constructor's first Grand Prix was at the Nürburgring in 1966?

10 Who was known as the 'Monza Gorilla'?
▼

11 Which 1985 race had to be postponed when the track surface broke up?

12 Only two German drivers have ever won a World Championship Grand Prix. Can you name them both?

13 Which landmark did Thierry Boutsen reach first: his first Grand Prix victory, or his 100th Grand Prix?

14 By the end of 1989, which team had enjoyed more Grand Prix victories in the 'eighties: Williams or McLaren?

15 How many different engine makers have supplied the power units for World Championship-winning *cars:* 6/8/10?

16 Which South African driver finished on the rostrum at his home Grand Prix in 1962?

RACE DAY

▲

1 What car was powered by an engine based on a Norton motorcycle engine?

2 Why was the 1989 Brazilian Grand Prix a landmark for Riccardo Patrese?

3 Who is the only man to have won three titles in three different cars?

4 Before Nigel Mansell arrived there, who was the last Briton to drive for Ferrari in a race?

5 In which two years were there 'All Turbo' grids?

6 In 1989, which two teams had to prequalify in Monaco but took points in the race?

7 In 1969 which two team-mates crashed on successive laps at the same place for the same reason?

8 When did Zakspeed score their first World Championship points?

9 How many Grands Prix did Chris Amon win?

10 Which two teams used six-wheel racing cars in the mid '70s?

11 Why was the launch of the Lotus 78 significant?

12 True or false? In 1984 the Turbo was so dominant that not one Ford Cosworth team scored a point?

13 What did Michele Alboreto and Nigel Mansell each achieve for the first time in 1984?

14 How many times did Brabham take pole position in 1984?

15 During John Watson's five years at McLaren, who were his team-mates?

16 When Richie Ginther won for Honda in Mexico in 1965, another American finished fifth in another Honda. Who?

PIT STOP (1):

GERMANY

1 Only once has the German GP been run at Avus. When — and where is it?

▼

2 When did Hockenheim first stage the German GP?

3 Who won that race?

4 Which Grand Prix driver was killed in a Formula Two race at Hockenheim?

5 Who won the last German GP at the Nürburgring?

6 Since the first German GP in 1951, there has been only one year without a German round of the Championship. Which?

7 What, to the nearest kilometre, was the length of the original Nürburgring lap?

8 Jim Clark won the German GP only once. In which year?

PIT STOP (2):

A YEAR IN FORMULA ONE: 1958

1 It was the first year of the Constructors' Championship. Who were the inaugural winners?

2 Who were the English trio of Vanwall drivers?

3 Indianapolis apart, there was one race where three American drivers finished in the top six. Where, and who were they?

4 It was also the year of the first Portuguese GP to count towards the World Championship. Where was it held?

5 One of the all-time greats drove his last Championship GP. Who and where?

6 Mike Hawthorn was World Champion but won only one race. Which?

7 Which well-known driver scored his first World Championship points, and where?

8 Sadly, two British drivers were killed in separate races. Who and where?

▼

PIT STOP (3):

TRACK RECORD

1 Name this track.

2 Who was first driver on pole there?

3 In the first Adelaide GP, who was disqualified for not respecting the start procedure?

4 Gerhard Berger led the 1988 race for Ferrari — until tangling with which car and driver?

5 Which other French driver scored the first points of his career there with Ligier?

6 Which stand-in also scored his first World Championship point there in 1987?

7 Why was Aryton Senna disqualified from second place that same year?

8 The 1986 race is famous for Nigel Mansell's spectacular retirement with a blown tyre. Which two other British drivers finished that race in the points?

PIT STOP (4):

THE WORLD CHAMPIONS

1 In 1975, in how many of the 14 races did Niki Lauda score?

2 Which World Champion stood 47 points behind the title leader at one point but still won it?

3 Which World Champion had a five-year wait between his first and second race victories?

4 Who was the first Champion in a British car?

5 In what position did James Hunt need to finish in Japan, last race of 1976, to win the title?

6 Where and when did the incomparable Fangio record his first World Championship race victory?

7 Mike Hawthorn was World Champion in 1958 with just one race win to his credit — Which?

8 Graham Hill was World Champion twice, in which two cars?

RESULTS

FIRST QUALIFYING

1 1968.
2 $50,000.
3 Niki Lauda, by half a point from McLaren team-mate Alain Prost in 1984.
4 Ten.
5 Martin Brundle — World Sportscar Champion of 1988.
6 ATS.
7 True — it was not until 1965 that Jim Clark broke the American post-war stranglehold.
8 Brabham-BMW.
9 Fifteen minutes.
10 Colin Chapman of Lotus.
11 True.
12 Twelve.
13 Teo Fabi, three times in 1985-86.
14 Longines, with the help of Olivetti computers.
15 Italy — the San Marino GP takes place at Imola.
16 Ayrton Senna.

SECOND QUALIFYING

1 Japanese GP at Suzuka.
2 Carlos Reutemann.
3 *To Hell and Back.*
4 Jean Alesi, for Tyrrell at the 1989 French Grand Prix.
5 Mexico 1987.
6 Mike Costin and Keith Duckworth.
7 Monaco 1983 — fifth for Tyrrell.
8 AGS.
9 Matra.
10 Italian Vittorio Brambilla.
11 The Belgian Grand Prix at Spa-Francorchamps.
12 Wolfgang von Trips and Jochen Mass.
13 His first victory: Canada 1989 preceded his 100th Grand Prix on his home circuit at Spa.
14 McLaren: 56-36 at time of writing, needs to be updated at season's end if we can.
15 Eight.
16 Tony Maggs (Cooper Climax).

RACE NINE

1 Vanwall.
2 His 177th — making him the most experienced Formula One racer of all time.
3 Fangio. In a Ferrari, a Mercedes and a Maserati.
4 Derek Bell.
5 1985/86.
6 Dallara and Brabham.
7 Graham Hill and Jochen Rindt (Lotus) at the Spanish GP; both suffered from aerofoil failure.
8 San Marino, 1987 (Martin Brundle was fifth).
9 None — in 96 races his best result was second (three times).
10 Tyrrell and March.
11 It heralded the 'Ground effect' era.
12 False. The gallant Arrows team managed to secure three points with it before their BMW Turbo came.
13 Pole position.
14 Nine — all by Nelson Piquet.
15 Patrick Tambay ('79), Alain Prost ('80), Andrea De Cesaris ('81), Niki Lauda ('82/'83).
16 Ronnie Bucknum (11 GPs 1964-66).

PIT STOP (1):

GERMANY

1 1959, Berlin.
2 1970.
3 Jochen Rindt (Lotus).
4 Jim Clark (7th April, 1968).
5 Michele Alboreto (Ferrari, 1985).
6 1960.
7 22.772 kms.
8 1965.

PIT STOP (2):

A YEAR IN F1 1958

1 Vanwall.
2 Stirling Moss, Tony Brooks, Stuart Lewis-Evans.
3 Italian GP, Monza: Phil Hill was third for Ferrari, Masten Gregory and Carroll Shelby co-drove a Maserati to fourth.
4 Oporto.
5 Juan Manuel Fangio, in France: he was fourth.
6 The French GP at Rheims.
7 Jack Brabham, fourth at Monaco.
8 Peter Collins at the Nürburgring, Stuart Lewis-Evans in Morocco.

PIT STOP (3):

TRACK RECORD

1 Adelaide.
2 Ayrton Senna in 1985 for Lotus.
3 Elio De Angelis.
4 The Ligier of René Arnoux.
5 Philippe Streiff in 1985.
6 Roberto Moreno, who took over the AGS drive.
7 Irregular brake ducts on his Lotus-Honda.
8 Martin Brundle (Tyrrell) was fourth, Johnny Dumfries (Lotus) was sixth.

PIT STOP (4):

THE WORLD CHAMPIONS

1 Twelve.
2 James Hunt in 1976.
3 Mario Andretti won in South Africa in 1971 but not again until Japan 1976.
4 Jack Brabham.
5 Third or better.
6 Monaco 1950.
7 French GP at Rheims.
8 BRM (1962) and Lotus (1968).

SCORE		
1st QUAL.		
2nd QUAL.		
RACE		
PITSTOP (1)		
PITSTOP (2)		
PITSTOP (3)		
PITSTOP (4)		
TOTAL		

HUNGARY

Marlboro
POP 84
OPEL
OPEL
Shell
POP 84
POP 84
POP 84
Philips Car Stereo

FIRST QUALIFYING

1 The driver line-up is John Watson and Alain Prost. Team and year?

2 Australia has had two great World Champions — but which had more Grand Prix wins, Brabham or Jones?

3 Which team in 1986 carried the name of a sponsor called Flying Tigers?

4 Who would be in the cockpit if you were looking at car number two in 1986?

7 Who celebrated his 100th Grand Prix at the final race of 1988?

8 Name the driver: started with Ensign in 1979, best result in 82 races was fourth, also drove for Arrows and Brabham, last Grand Prix Belgium 1986.

9 Which fuel do Ferrari use?

10 What was former World Champion Emerson Fittipaldi's brother's first name?
▼

13 Where did Britain's Julian Bailey make his Grand Prix debut?
▼

14 Which was Martin Brundle's single Grand Prix drive for Williams?

5 What nationality is former Grand Prix driver Chico Serra?

6 Which recent Grand Prix star was nicknamed Prince Charming?

11 Which British driver deputised for a compatriot in 1989 and joined forces with him for 1990?

12 Which of the Rodriguez brothers was the elder?

15 Who achieved his first rostrum finish at the 1989 Brazilian Grand Prix?

16 Which famous team boss wrote a book called *My Terrible Joys*?

SECOND QUALIFYING

1 Stefan Johansson was the lone Swede in Formula One in 1989. Name any two Swedish GP drivers before him?

2 Who drove the oddly-named McLaren Serenissima in the 1966 British GP?

3 Which driver made a 'token' appearance in his first GP in Belgium in 1974?

7 At which race did Chris Amon score the first of his five pole positions?

8 Which driver returned to Formula One at Detroit in 1988 and scored his own — and his team's — first World Championship point?

9 Who was the only non-Ferrari driver to win a GP in 1961?

▼

12 Who replaced World Champion Denny Hulme in the Brabham line-up for 1968?

13 Which team had a 1-2-3-4 at the 1955 British GP?

14 With which team did Stirling Moss begin his illustrious career?

15 There was just one World Championship Pescara GP — in which year?

4 How many different teams have had a World Champion?

5 At which circuit would you find Dingle Dell?

6 In 1989 whose engine did Zakspeed use?

10 Which is Porche's only Grand Prix win as a constructor?

11 Which driver has won the World Championship by the greatest margin?

16 1970, as everyone recalls, saw Jochen Rindt proclaimed the posthumous World Champion. Which two other drivers lost their lives in that sad year?

RACE DAY

▲

1 Which two concepts were the Connaught team pioneering in 1954?

2 Which driver raced with a deformed hand?

3 Which was the first company to sponsor the British GP?

4 1958 saw Mike Hawthorn beat Stirling Moss to the title. How many races did they win?

5 What is the average audience for a Grand Prix (in terms of TV figures): 25/75/90 million?

6 Who was killed in a Vanwall the very last time that team appeared at a Grand Prix?

7 Which team, with a famous name, re-entered Formula One in 1987 and scored its first points at Monaco?

8 In which year did sponsorship first appear on cars?

9 What was the first car to appear in the colours of its sponsor?

10 Who drove the first rear engined car since the days of the Auto Union team?

11 How many German drivers took part in the 1989 German GP?

12 Which team did Marlboro sponsor before McLaren?

13 How was it that Giuseppe Farina managed to come second *and* third in the 1955 Argentine GP?

14 Which was the first GP car to feature the engine as a stressed part of the chassis?

15 Who was the first Japanese driver to take part in a Grand Prix?

16 What year saw the first appearance of aerofoils? ▼

PIT STOP (1):

HUNGARY

1 In which year was the Hungarian GP first held?

2 Drivers of only two nationalities have won in Hungary. Which?

3 Which engine powered the first Hungarian winner?

4 Who was the best-placed non-turbo driver in Hungary in 1988?

▼

5 Who took pole position at the Hungaroring in 1989?

6 Which driver has never been out of the top three in Hungary?

7 Which British driver scored his first points of 1986 in Hungary?

8 Why might Nigel Mansell say 'Nuts' to Hungary?

PIT STOP (2):

A YEAR IN FORMULA ONE: 1968

1 Who was runner-up to Graham Hill in the Drivers' Championship?

2 Ferrari won only one race. Which, by whom?

▼

3 Name the two teams for which Dan Gurney drove.

4 Jochen Rindt secured the first of his ten pole positions. Where?

5 What was significant about the South African GP?

6 Another great driver scored his last Grand Prix victory. Who and where?

7 What else was noteworthy about that result?

8 A current Formula One team manager was on the front row for the British GP. Can you name him?

PIT STOP (3):

TEAM TALK: TYRRELL

1 When did Jonathan Palmer first score points for Tyrrell?

2 Which race did Ken Tyrrell win with a March chassis?

3 How many race victories has Ken Tyrrell enjoyed as a Formula One team manager: 27/33/35?

4 What was Jody Scheckter's first win in a Tyrrell?

5 What was the innovative Tyrrell six-wheeler designated?
▼

6 Who stood in for Jackie Stewart in the Tyrrell-Matra at the 1968 Monaco Grand Prix?

7 Where and when did a Tyrrell, properly so called, make its debut?

8 What was the last race Stefan Bellof drove for Tyrrell?

PIT STOP (4):

RULES AND REGULATIONS

▲

1 In which year did British fans first see a green light start their Grand Prix?

2 What was the ground clearance height imposed by FISA in 1981?

3 What was the unsupercharged limit for a Grand Prix car up to 1952?

4 In 1987 what was the limit on turbo pressure?

5 At race start, what is the maximum time between red and green lights being switched on?

6 What was banned after Niki Lauda's dominant victory in the 1978 Swedish GP?

7 In which year were skirts outlawed — on the track?

8 Which year first saw limitations imposed on fuel capacity?

RESULTS

FIRST QUALIFYING

1 McLaren, 1980.
2 Sir Jack had 14 to Alan's 12.
3 Benetton.
4 Keke Rosberg (McLaren).
5 Brazilian.
6 Patrick Tambay of France.
7 Derek Warwick.
8 Marc Surer of Switzerland.
9 Agip.
10 Wilson — he took part in 36 Grands Prix.
11 Martin Donnelly.
12 Pedro was born in 1940, Ricardo in 1942.
13 San Marino 1988, for Tyrrell.
14 Belgium 1988 — he finished ninth.
15 Mauricio Gugelmin (Leyton House March) was third.
16 Enzo Ferrari.

SECOND QUALIFYING

1 Jo Bonnier, Slim Borgudd, Gunnar Nilsson, Ronnie Peterson, Reine Wisell.
2 Bruce McLaren.
3 Tom Pryce — in a Token Ford.
4 Twelve.
5 Brands Hatch. It is part of the full GP circuit.
6 Yamaha.
7 Spain 1968 — Ferrari.
8 Pierluigi Martini, sixth for Minardi.
9 Stirling Moss, who won in a Lotus in Monaco and Germany.
10 French GP 1962, by Dan Gurney.
11 Jackie Stewart, 29 points ahead of Ronnie Peterson in 1971.
12 Jochen Rindt.
13 Mercedes.
14 HWM.
15 1957 — winner Stirling Moss (Vanwall).
16 Bruce McLaren and Piers Courage.

RACE TEN

1 Fuel injection and disc brakes.
2 Archie Scott-Brown.
3 British Wool.
4 Hawthorn 1, Moss 4.
5 On average 90 million watch a race on TV.
6 Stuart Lewis-Evans (Morocco, 1958).
7 March.
8 1968.
9 The Gold Leaf Lotus.
10 Jack Brabham.
11 None — they all failed to qualify.
12 BRM.
13 He shared the cars that came second and third with three other drivers!
14 Lancia D50.
15 Masahiro Hasemi: Japanese GP, 1976, Kojima-Ford.
16 1968.

PIT STOP (1):

HUNGARY

1 1986.
2 Brazilian (Piquet twice, Senna once), and British (Mansell once).
3 Renault turbo.
4 Mauricio Gugelmin (March).
5 Riccardo Patrese (Williams).
6 Ayrton Senna (2nd-2nd-1st-2nd).
7 Johnny Dumfries (Lotus, fifth).
8 A loose wheel nut cost him the chance of victory in 1987.

PIT STOP (2):

A YEAR IN F1 1968

1 Jackie Stewart, 36 points to Hill's 48.
2 French GP, Jackie Ickx.
3 Eagle and McLaren.
4 French GP at Rouen in a Brabham-Repco.
5 It brought the last victory of Jim Clark's career.
6 Bruce McLaren at the Belgian GP.
7 It was the first victory for McLaren as constructor.
8 Jackie Oliver, now Arrows team manager, in a Lotus.

PIT STOP (3):

TEAM TALK: TYRRELL

1 Australia, 1987, when he was fourth.
2 Spanish GP 1970.
3 33.
4 Swedish Grand Prix, 1974.
5 Project 34.
6 Johnny Servoz-Gavin.
7 Canadian GP, 1970 — and Stewart put it on pole.
8 Dutch GP, 1985.

PIT STOP (4):

RULES AND REGULATIONS

1 1975.
2 Six centimetres.
3 4.5 litres.
4 Four atmospheres.
5 Seven seconds.
6 The large rear fan that generated downforce.
7 1981.
8 1984.

SCORE		
1st QUAL.		
2nd QUAL.		
RACE		
PITSTOP (1)		
PITSTOP (2)		
PITSTOP (3)		
PITSTOP (4)		
TOTAL		

BELGIUM

FIRST QUALIFYING

1 Two drivers each finished second on three successive occasions in 1989. Who?

2 How many Swedish Grands Prix have there been?

3 Who wore this helmet in 1989?

▼

4 At which 1989 race did Christian Danner score his first points since 1986?

5 Which drivers, belonging to the same team, crashed into each other soon after the start of the 1987 Belgian GP?

6 What were the principal colours of John Watson's racing helmet?

7 Which season has been Derek Warwick's most successful in terms of points scored?

8 What did the Williams that won in Canada in 1989 have in common with the Lotus that won in Detroit in 1986?

9 Name three of the four teams which did not score constructors' points in the 1989 season.

10 Who deputised for Pierluigi Martini in the Minardi at Suzuka in 1989?

11 Which famous team manager used to rejoice in the nickname 'Chopper'?

12 Only once has Eddie Cheever started a Grand Prix from the front row. Which?

13 Which current Grand Prix circuit is on an island?

14 When Judd supplied engines for the first time in 1988, Lotus and Williams were two of their teams. Which was the third?

15 Which driver was nicknamed Rocky?

16 When was the last US GP staged at Long Beach?

▼

SECOND QUALIFYING

1 Who won — and lost — the 1985 San Marino Grand Prix — and why?

2 Where and when did Derek Warwick make his Grand Prix debut?

3 Who preceeded Murray Walker as the BBC's motor racing commentator?

4 No team has yet (end 1989) managed one hundred Grand Prix wins — true or false?

5 Name the driver and this event.
▼

6 Which is the only pole position ever claimed by a Honda?

7 As Constructors, Renault only enjoyed one 1-2 finish. When and where?

8 Which was the last season in which Englebert supplied Formula One tyres?

9 Which driver had to be flown home in a special medical jet after a pre-season accident in testing in 1989?

10 Which team had more pole positions in the seventies: Ferrari or Lotus?

11 Why would McLaren rather forget the 1983 Monaco Grand Prix?

12 What was the nationality of the driver who replaced Yannick Dalmas at Larrousse for the 1989 French GP?

13 What was the last race in which James Hunt scored World Championship points?

14 Who was the last driver on pole position in a BRM?

15 On how many GP circuits has Nigel Mansell won more than once?

16 What was the last race with a Belgian driver on pole?

RACE DAY

1 What did Johnny Herbert do in Brazil in 1989 that hadn't been done since 1980?

2 Who was the last man to achieve that feat before Herbert?

3 Where did J. M. Fangio win his last race?

4 How did the phrase 'Pole Position' originate?

5 Who was the only driver to score a hat-trick of victories when the US Grand Prix was run at Watkins Glen?

6 Whose Lotus crashed into the harbour during the 1965 Monaco Grand Prix?

7 Juan Manuel Fangio raced in 51 Grands Prix. How many times from Pole Position?

8 Which World Champion continued racing for many years and at the age of 51 raced at Indianapolis?

9 Between 1952/3 how many races did Alberto Ascari win on the trot?

10 What engine won Monaco four times in a row?

11 Which team has taken part in most GPs without a win?

12 Alan Rees has had his initials as part of two teams. Which ones?

13 In the two seasons of 1987/8 there were 32 GPs. On how many occasions did the front row of the grid contain the same make of car. Less than 10, 10-20, more than 20?

14 What happened at the 1961 Belgium GP that can never happen again?

15 Which team took Arrows to court claiming that the car was a direct copy?

16 Mario Andretti won twice on only one circuit — which?
▼

PIT STOP (1):

BELGIUM

1 Name the three circuits on which the Belgian GP has been run?

2 When was the last race over the full Spa circuit?

3 Who won it?

4 Which two drivers came to blows on and off the track in the 1987 Belgian GP?

5 Why was Alain Prost's 1987 victory so significant?

6 How did the 1989 Belgian GP give Lotus an unhappy first?

7 Who won the last Belgian GP at Zolder?

8 What is the name of the fearsome corner at the bottom of the former start line at Spa?

▼

PIT STOP (2):

A YEAR IN FORMULA ONE: 1976

1 Which two teams used Carlos Reutemann's services?

2 Who sponsored the Penske driven by John Watson?

3 Ligier entered the field with the JS5. What did the initials stand for?

▼

4 Which was James Hunt's first victory of the season?

5 Jody Scheckter recorded his final win for Tyrrell. Where?

6 At which circuit did Niki Lauda have a near-fatal accident?

7 Lauda went into the history books for having the courage to retire from a rain-lashed Japanese GP. But who was the other driver who did the same?

8 Hunt and Watson apart, another British driver scored World Championship points that year. Name him and his car.

PIT STOP (3):

TEAM TALK: LOTUS

1 What was significant about the USA GP in 1961 to the Lotus outfit?

2 In 1962 Lotus started with one engine and ended the season with another. Name them.

▼

3 The first time Hockenheim hosted the German GP it was won by Lotus. Who drove that day?

4 Five engines have been used to power Lotus to a total of 79 victories. Name them.

5 Which Lotus driver spent his entire 72 race career with them?

6 What was Nigel Mansell's best position in five years at Lotus?

7 Who assumed overall managerial responsibility at Team Lotus when Peter Warr left in 1989?

8 Which driver replaced the injured Jochen Rindt in the Lotus team at Monaco in 1968?

PIT STOP (4):

DESIGNERS

1 Which designer followed Nelson Piquet from Williams to Lotus?

2 Who re-designed the 1954 2-litre Vanwall into a 4-cylinder winner for Stirling Moss?

▼

3 Name the designer who left Arrows at the end of 1989 to join Jaguar?

4 Jochen Rindt won four races in 1970 in the Lotus 1972. Who designed the car?

5 Which famous designer announced a link-up with Benetton during 1989?

6 Who has designed all the Minardi cars?

7 Which designer is the son of a former Ferrari and Alfa Romeo mechanic?

8 Ingeniere Dallara was responsible for which shortlived design?

RESULTS

FIRST QUALIFYING

1 Alain Prost (Brazil, San Marino, Monaco); Riccardo Patrese (Mexico, USA, Canada)
2 Six: 1973-1978.
3 Stefan Johansson.
4 Phoenix, US GP — he was fourth.
5 Philippe Streiff and Jonathan Palmer (Tyrrell).
6 Silver and orange.
7 1984: 23 points, seventh in the Championship (he was seventh in 1988 but with 17).
8 A Renault engine.
9 Osella, Coloni, EuroBrun, Zakspeed.
10 Paolo Barilla of Italy.
11 Ken Tyrrell, who was once a timber merchant.
12 French GP, 1983 — in a Renault.
13 Circuit Gilles Villeneuve is on Montreal's Ile Notre Dame.
14 Ligier.
15 Keke Rosberg.
16 1983 — winner was John Watson (McLaren).

SECOND QUALIFYING

1 Alain Prost, whose McLaren was two kilos under minimum weight.
2 Las Vegas, 1981 in a Toleman.
3 Raymond Baxter — amongst others who worked for the BBC were John Bolster and Max Robertson.
4 True — Ferrari, with 97 are closest.
5 Jean-Louis Schlesser, Italian Grand Prix, 1988.
6 Italian Grand Prix 1968 with John Surtees at the wheel.
7 French Grand Prix at Le Castellet 1982; Arnoux and Prost drove that day.
8 1958.
9 Philippe Streiff, whose AGS crashed violently while testing at Rio.
10 Ferrari — 41 to 37.
11 Niki Lauda and John Watson both failed to qualify.
12 Eric Bernard is French.
13 French Grand Prix 1978, when he was third in a McLaren.
14 Clay Regazzoni at the Argentine Grand Prix of 1973.
15 Two Paul Ricard and Brands Hatch.
16 Italian Grand Prix 1972, with Jackie Ickx appropriately enough in a Ferrari.

RACE ELEVEN

1 He scored points in his first World Championship race.
2 Alain Prost (Argentine GP 1980).
3 German GP at Nürburgring in 1957 (Maserati).
4 From the practice of starting alongside the starter's pole.
5 Graham Hill, 1963-4-5 all for BRM.
6 Paul Hawkins.
7 28.
8 Giuseppe Farina.
9 Two — for Ferrari.
10 BRM V8, 1963-4-5-6.
11 Arrows 183 to the end of 1989.
12 M(AR)ch and (AR)rows.
13 It happened 17 times.
14 A team, in this case Ferrari, took the first four places.
15 Shadow.
16 Jarama, Spain, in 1977 and 1978.

PIT STOP (1):

BELGIUM

1 Spa-Francorchamps, Nivelles and Zolder.
2 1970.
3 Pedro Rodriguez, BRM.
4 Aryton Senna and Nigel Mansell.
5 He equalled Jackie Stewart's record of 27 victories.
6 First time neither car managed to qualify.
7 Michele Alboreto, Ferrari, 1984.
8 Eau Rouge.

PIT STOP (2):

A YEAR IN F1 1976

1 Ferrari and Martini Brabham.
2 First National City Bank.
3 Jo Schlesser, Guy Ligier's friend killed in the 1968 French GP.
4 Spanish GP at Jarama.
5 Swedish GP, Anderstorp.
6 Nürburgring.
7 Carlos Pace (Martini Brabham).
8 Tom Pryce, Shadow.

PIT STOP (3):

TEAM TALK: LOTUS

1 First *team* win. Although Moss had won twice in a private Lotus.
2 Coventry Climax, and later the BRM.
3 Jochen Rindt in 1970.
4 Ford/Climax/Renault/Honda/BRM.
5 Jim Clark.
6 Third (on four occasions).
7 Tony Rudd.
8 Dickie Attwood.

PIT STOP (4):

DESIGNERS

1 Frank Dernie.
2 Colin Chapman and Frank Costin.
3 Ross Brawn.
4 Maurice Phillippe.
5 John Barnard.
6 Giacomo Caliri.
7 Mauro Forghieri, whose father Reclus worked on the pre-war Alfa Romeo 158s.
8 The 1970 De Tomaso.

SCORE		
1st QUAL.		
2nd QUAL.		
RACE		
PITSTOP (1)		
PITSTOP (2)		
PITSTOP (3)		
PITSTOP (4)		
TOTAL		

RACETWELVE

ITALY

FIRST QUALIFYING

▲

1 It's 1954, and it's obviously a Ferrari. Who is at the wheel?

2 How many drivers made their Formula One debut in the 1989 French Grand Prix?

3 During the 'eighties the Spanish Grand Prix has been won twice by only one driver. Who?

4 Which circuit has a feature called the Rivazza?

5 What nationality is Roberto Moreno?

6 How many times did Detroit stage a Grand Prix?

7 How many times did Ayrton Senna win in Detroit?

8 Where, in 1989, did a Minardi lead a Grand Prix?

9 How many times have McLaren been World Champion Constructors?

10 Which was the first Grand Prix contested by a Ford-engined car?

11 No team has achieved a hat-trick of Constructors' World Championships since Ferrari in 1975-6-7: true or false?

12 Which Spaniard has taken part in more Grands Prix than any of his compatriots?

13 How many times was pole position specialist Ayrton placed in that spot in 1987?

14 Nigel Mansell was black-flagged twice in 1989. Where?

15 At which race did Alain Prost secure his first World Championship?

16 For how many Formula One teams has Martin Brundle driven?

▼

SECOND QUALIFYING

1 The 1982 Belgian Grand Prix was overshadowed by the death, in qualifying, of Gilles Villeneuve. Who eventually won the race?

▼

2 What colours predominated on Gilles Villeneuve's helmet?

3 Former World Champion Denny Hulme took pole position just once in his 112-race career. Where and when?

4 Whose entry into Formula One was aided by Abba?

5 What was the best finish of Mark Donohue's tragically short career?

6 There have been just two Grand Prix drivers whose surname began with Z. Can you name either?

7 Apart from the famous Nürburgring, which other former World Championship circuit had a feature called the Karusell?

8 Which driver bravely pulled Niki Lauda from his blazing Ferrari at the Nürburgring in 1976?

▼

9 Huub Rothengatter apart, can you name another Dutch Grand Prix driver?

10 What was the designation of the first Brabham GP car?

11 Tom Pryce was on pole position at the 1975 British Grand Prix. Which was the only other front-row start of his career?

12 Who was Derek Warwick's team-mate when Toleman entered Formula One in 1981?

13 In how many races did Michele Alboreto compete for Tyrrell in 1989?

14 With which famous British team do you associate the name of Raymond Mays?

15 Which famous car was nicknamed 'The Stackpipe'?

16 Tiff Needell is now a well-known commentator. Which was his one and only Grand Prix?

RACE DAY

▲

1 Who was awarded the George Medal for saving Clay Regazzoni's life at the 1973 South African GP?

2 Which constructor boasts the highest average of points scored per GP: McLaren, Vanwall or Ferrari?

3 How did Brabham cause a stir at the 1978 Swedish GP?

4 Which well-known driver was nicknamed Lolo?

5 AGS is a prominent French team. What do the initials stand for?

6 Shadow boasted just one Grand Prix win: where, when, who?

7 Ferraris finished 1-2 in the 1966 Italian GP. Who drove?

8 At which race did Niki Lauda return to the cockpit after his horrific accident at the Nürburgring?

9 In which year was the first 100 mph average lap speed recorded at Silverstone: 1951/1956/1961?

10 Only one driver managed to finish all ten World Championship races in 1964. Who?

11 It is 1952 and you are watching a dice between a Tipo 500 and an A6 GCM. How are the cars better known?

12 In 1971 which driver scored four second places in his first season?

13 Which was the final World Championship season for the famous Coopers?

14 From 1960-1962 the winner of the Italian GP was called Hill. How did Phil and Graham divide the spoils?

15 Sadly Germany lost three of its potentially great Formula One stars in the 80s. Can you name them?

16 Which was the only World Championship race, apart from Indianapolis, Alberto Ascari failed to win in 1952? ▶

PIT STOP (1):

ITALY

1 When was the first Italian GP staged?

2 Which French driver helped Ferrari win at Monza in 1988?

3 How did Alain Prost incur the wrath of McLaren team manager Ron Dennis at Monza in 1989?

4 What is the name given to the fanatical Ferrari fans?

5 Fangio was the first non-Italian winner at Monza. When?

6 Which current driver has won the Italian GP most often?

7 Which much-loved Ferrari driver died at Monza in 1961?

8 In which year was the famous banked section at Monza last used in a World Championship race?

▼

PIT STOP (2):

A YEAR IN FORMULA ONE: 1985

1 Which team was forced to pull out before the end of the season because of a cash shortage?

2 Ferrari had two wins before their long barren spell started. Where?

3 Three drivers raced in McLarens. Who?

4 At which race did Nigel Mansell have a severe accident in practice and not take the start?

5 Why were Silverstone officials red-faced?

6 Which circuit staged the Grand Prix of Europe?

7 It is well known as the year of Ayrton Senna's first victory, in Portugal. But where was his second?

8 It was also Nigel Mansell's first season as a racewinner. The first came at Brands Hatch — and the second?

▼

PIT STOP (3):

TRACK RECORD

1 At which circuit are these girls?
▼

2 In which year did it stage the Italian GP?

3 What is the name of the acute left-hander after the start?

4 Who was the first winner of a GP at this circuit?

5 Who is the only Italian to have won there?

6 Italy is always an impassioned arena for the Grand Prix drivers. Why was this track especially so for Patrick Tambay in 1983?

7 Which driver, a year earlier, defied team protocol to deny Villeneuve victory there?

8 In 1988 the car in fourth place was the first atmospheric runner to score points that season. Whose was it?

PIT STOP (4):

PICTORIAL POSER

1 ▲ Name the circuit.

2 There are two makes of car on the front row. Name them.

3 Name two of the three front-row drivers.

4 How many times did the circuit host the French GP?

5 Which was the last year for this circuit as a World Championship venue?

6 Who won that race?

7 What was the name of the hairpin?

8 Who won the race pictured here?

RESULTS

FIRST QUALIFYING

1. Mike Hawthorn.
2. Five: Alesi, Bernard, Donnelly, Gachot, Pirro.
3. Ayrton Senna: 1986 and 1989.
4. Imola, home of the San Marino GP.
5. Brazilian.
6. Seven: 1982-88 inclusive.
7. Three: 1986/7/8.
8. Portugal, when Pierluigi Martini was leader for half a lap.
9. Five: 1974/84/85/88/89.
10. US GP, Watkins Glen 1963.
11. True: Williams, Ferrari themselves and McLaren have all done it twice in succession but not three times.
12. Luis Perez Sala.
13. Just once — for the San Marino GP at Imola (Lotus).
14. In Canada and Portugal.
15. European GP 1985 at Brands Hatch by finishing fourth.
16. Four: Tyrrell, Zakspeed, Brabham — and one race for Williams.

SECOND QUALIFYING

1. John Watson (McLaren).
2. Dark blue and red.
3. South African GP 1973 (McLaren).
4. Slim Borgudd of Sweden.
5. Third Mosport, Canadian GP 1971 (McLaren).
6. Renzo Zorzi (Italy) and Ricardo Zunino (Argentina).
7. Anderstorp in Sweden.
8. Arturo Merzario.
9. Gijs van Lennep and Jan Lammers.
10. BT3, which made its debut at the Nürburgring in 1962.
11. Monaco 1975 (Shadow).
12. Brian Henton.
13. Five: he did not qualify at Imola, left after round six at Montreal.
14. BRM.
15. The 1962 World Championship-winning BRM, because of its original eight swept-up exhaust pipes.
16. Belgian GP 1980, in an Ensign: he retired with engine failure.

RACE TWELVE

1. Mike Hailwood.
2. Vanwall.
3. By introducing the 'fan car' with an extractor mounted vertically behind the gearbox — and seeing Niki Lauda drive it to victory.
4. Carlos Reutemann.
5. Automobile Gonfaronaises Sportives.
6. Austria 1977, Alan Jones.
7. First Ludovico Scarfiotti, second Mike Parkes.
8. Italian GP 1976 — and he finished fourth.
9. 1951: by eventual racewinner Froilan Gonzalez (Ferrari) in practice.
10. Richie Ginther (BRM).
11. Ferrari and Maserati.
12. Ronnie Peterson.
13. 1968.
14. Phil won 1960-61, Graham 1962.
15. Stefan Bellof, Rolf Stommelin, Manfred Winkelhock.
16. The first one, the Swiss GP won by Ferrari team-mate Taruffi.

PIT STOP (1):

ITALY

1. 1950.
2. Jean-Louis Schlesser, who tangled with the leading McLaren of Ayrton Senna.
3. By dropping the winner's trophy to the fans.
4. Tifosi.
5. 1953 (Maserati).
6. Nelson Piquet — four times.
7. Wolfgang von Trips.
8. 1961.

PIT STOP (2):

A YEAR IN F1 1985

1. RAM.
2. Canada and Germany.
3. Niki Lauda, Alain Prost and . . . John Watson.
4. French GP.
5. Because they waved the chequered flag a lap early.
6. Brands Hatch.
7. Belgium.
8. South Africa.

PIT STOP (3):

TRACK RECORD

1. Imola: Autodromo Dino e Enzo Ferrari.
2. 1980.
3. (Curva) Tosa.
4. Nelson Piquet in 1981 for Brabham.
5. Elio De Angelis, Lotus 1985.
6. He drove Ferrari 27 — the number of the late, much-loved Gilles Villeneuve — to victory there.
7. Didier Pironi (Ferrari).
8. Thierry Boutsen's Benetton-Ford.

PIT STOP (4):

PICTORIAL POSER

1. Rheims, France.
2. Two Alfa Romeos and a Ferrari.
3. Ascari (Ferrari), Farina and Fangio.
4. Eleven.
5. 1966.
6. Jack Brabham in a Brabham-Repco.
7. Thillois.
8. Fagioli and Fangio in a shared Alfa-Romeo after Fangio's own car had been delayed by a lengthy pit-stop.

SCORE		
1st QUAL.		
2nd QUAL.		
RACE		
PITSTOP (1)		
PITSTOP (2)		
PITSTOP (3)		
PITSTOP (4)		
TOTAL		

PORTUGAL

FIRST QUALIFYING

1 Who scored his first Grand Prix win in Canada in 1989?

2 What do these current Formula One drivers: Prost, Alesi, Herbert, Brundle — have in common?

3 Which World Championship venue boasts a fearsome right-hander called the Bosch-Kurve?

▼

4 Two teams used V10 engines in 1989: which?

5 Who was the only driver with a 100% record in pre-qualifying in 1989?

6 How many forward speeds were there on Ferrari's 1989 gearbox?

7 What is Nelson Piquet's real name?

8 Who scored his first ever 'fastest lap' at Australia 1989?

▲

9 Who was Team Boss of Onyx?

10 In which city was the Montjuich circuit?

11 Who was fined for using the wrong tyres in prequalifying at Estoril in 1989?

12 Which famous driver had a helmet painted in the colours of Wellington School?

13 Which of the 16 races is run at the highest altitude?

14 Riccardo Patrese has driven in more Grands Prix than anyone else. How many times has he failed to qualify? 0/5/10.

15 Alain Prost has never finished outside the top five in the Drivers' World Championship: true or false?

16 At which 1989 race did Honda celebrate their 50th victory: Brazil/Germany/Belgium?

SECOND QUALIFYING

1 Where did Lorenzo Bandini achieve his one and only Grand Prix victory?

2 What, in Grand Prix history, was the Concorde Agreement?

3 For which team was Spaniard Francesco Godia an occasional competitor?

4 Which former Tyrrell, Ensign, Williams driver had a black helmet with a yellow arrow?

5 Australian, born 1943; best result was third for Brabham, Austria 1971; he drove for Surtees too, among others: who is he?

6 Which make of car was raced by no fewer than seven drivers in 1970?

7 Where did the Lamborghini V12 engine score its first World Championship point?

8 Which Ferrari drivers scored a 1-2 success in the 1972 German Grand Prix?

9 Which former World Championship circuit had a corner called Bethlehem?

10 Give the surnames of two men called Jean-Pierre who drove Tyrrells in the 'seventies.

▼

11 Which was the first season that saw a Ferrari victory in the USA? 1961-1969-1975?

12 At which race did Graham Hill announce his retirement?

13 How did Vittorio Brambilla meet both triumph and disaster at the 1975 Austrian GP?

14 What did Lotus, McLaren and Matra all try out in 1969?

15 Which driver announced his retirement in 1989 after scoring just two points since 1981?

16 Which was the one season in which De Tomaso cars competed?

RACE DAY

1 Which royal driver took part in the first five seasons of the World Championship?

2 Which current team manager scored one point as a driver in 1967?

3 How many races did Emerson Fittipaldi win in a McLaren?

4 Which driver holds the record for most wins in his home country's GP?

5 What nationality was former BRM driver Howden Ganley?
▼

6 Who stood in for Patrick Tambay at the 1986 Detroit GP?

7 Which car was nicknamed the 'Lobster Claw'?

8 What was the minimum weight of a Grand Prix car in 1988?

9 Who was the first man to win a race at the wheel of a BRM?

10 What was completely new on the McLaren at the British GP in 1989?

11 Which was the final victory of Stirling Moss's brilliant career?

▲

12 Where did Ronnie Peterson claim the last pole position of his career?

13 Which driver gave Brabham their first World Championship victory?

14 Jonathan Palmer set fastest race lap for the first time in his career in 1989. At which race?

15 How many victories had Goodyear advanced by the end of '89.

16 John Surtees clinched the 1964 World Championship with second place in Mexico. Which other two drivers were in title contention at the start of that race?

PIT STOP (1):

PORTUGAL

1 When did Portugal first join the World Championship?

2 At which circuits before Estoril?

3 When did Estoril first stage the Portuguese race?

4 True or false: the 1988 Portuguese GP was started three times?

▼

5 For what offence did Nigel Mansell incur disqualification in 1989?

6 Which British driver has twice won in Portugal?

7 Who took pole position for the first time in his career in Portugal in 1987?

8 Which driver claimed his career-best result in Portugal in 1988?

PIT STOP (2):

A YEAR IN FORMULA ONE 1959

1 Why was the Dutch GP at Zandvoort so important to British motor racing followers?

2 The German GP was held for the first — and last — time at a particular circuit. Which?

3 Aston Martin were still in Formula One. Who was their English driver?

4 The first race of the season at Monaco brought the first victory for a driver who would become a Grand Prix legend. Who?

5 The last race was the US GP. Where?

6 How many races did Stirling Moss win?

7 Ferrari were conspicuous by their absence from the British GP. Why?

8 Jack Brabham won the world title by finishing . . . where, in the last race of the season?

▼

PIT STOP (3):

TEAM TALK: MARCH

1 March are now well-established again in Formula One, but when was the team's first-ever GP?

2 At the end of which season did they withdraw?

3 A March car won the Spanish GP in 1970, but not with a March team driver aboard. How so?

4 Who were the drivers when March made their first GP comeback in 1981?
▼

5 In the final year of that second spell in Formula One Kenny Acheson took part in just one GP. Where?

6 When March again returned to the GP fold in 1987, why did Ivan Capelli not start the Rio race?

7 Where did Capelli score the team's only point in that season?

8 March are expected to be racewinners in the near future, but where, when and by whom was the team's last win?

PIT STOP (4):

THE WORLD CHAMPIONS

1 What was the title of Sir Jack Brabham's autobiography?

2 Which World Champion made a complete recovery from a horrific accident in a Lola sportscar at Mosport?

3 Which was Denny Hulme's last GP victory?

4 Keke Rosberg was Champion in 1982. How many points had he scored the previous year?

5 Which World Champion had a bad accident at the 1969 US GP?

6 Who have been Austria's two World Champions?

7 Which World Champion was originally a mechanic for Carlos Pace?
▼

8 Which initial in total of surnames of World Champions is the most successful?

RESULTS

FIRST QUALIFYING

1 Thierry Boutsen.
2 They each scored points in their first Grand Prix, though Brundle's were later discounted.
3 The Oesterreichring, Austria.
4 McLaren (Honda) and Williams (Renault).
5 Stefano Modena (Brabham).
6 Seven.
7 Nelson Souto Mayor.
8 Satoru Nakajima.
9 Mike Earle.
10 Barcelona: it hosted the Spanish Grand Prix in 1969, 1971, 1973 and 1975.
11 Yannick Dalmas (AGS).
12 James Hunt.
13 The Mexican GP (approx. 7,000 ft. above sea level).
14 Never.
15 False: he was 15th in his first season, 1980.
16 Belgium.

SECOND QUALIFYING

1 Zeltweg (Austria) 1964 in a Ferrari.
2 The compromise that ended controversy between FOCA and FISA in the early 'eighties.
3 Maserati — 13 times 1951-58.
4 Derek Daly.
5 Tim Schenken.
6 March — two works cars and five privateers.
7 Portuguese GP 1989, Alliot driving.
8 Jackie Ickx and Clay Regazzoni — in that order!
9 Bremgarten (Switzerland).
10 Jarier and Jabouille.
11 1975: Niki Lauda at Watkins Glen.
12 British GP 1975.
13 He won the race — his only victory — but crashed while celebrating in the cockpit!
14 Four-wheel drive.
15 Piercarlo Ghinzani.
16 1970.

RACE THIRTEEN

1 Prince Bira (Birabongse Bhanuban) of Thailand.
2 Guy Ligier, then with Brabham.
3 Five (1974-75).
4 Jim Clark, winner of the British GP five times 1962-67.
5 New Zealander.
6 Eddie Cheever.
7 Brabham BT34 (1971), which had radiators in extended pods at the front.
8 500 kg atmospheric. 540 kg turbocharged.
9 Jo Bonnier (Dutch GP 1959).
10 A transverse gearbox.
11 German GP Nürburgring 1961 (Lotus Climax).
12 The Oesterreichring: 1978 — and he won the race.
13 Dan Gurney (French GP 1964).
14 The Canadian GP.
15 216.
16 Jim Clark and Graham Hill.

PIT STOP (1):

PORTUGAL

1 1958.
2 Oporto and Monsanto.
3 1984.
4 True.
5 Reversing in the pit lane under his own power.
6 Stirling Moss.
7 Gerhard Berger.
8 Ivan Capelli.

PIT STOP (2):

A YEAR IN F1 1959

1 It brought the first victory for BRM.
2 AVUS, near Berlin.
3 Roy Salvadori.
4 Jack Brabham.
5 Sebring.
6 Two: Portugal and Italy.
7 They were hit by labour disputes in Italy.
8 Fourth.

PIT STOP (3):

TEAM TALK: MARCH

1 South Africa, 1970: Amon, Siffert and Andretti drove.
2 1977.
3 It was Jackie Stewart in the Ken Tyrrell-entered Elf March.
4 Derek Daly and Eliseo Salazar.
5 South Africa: he was classified 12th.
6 Shortage of engines.
7 He was sixth at Monaco.
8 Italy, 1976, Ronnie Peterson.

PIT STOP (4):

THE WORLD CHAMPIONS

1 *When the Flag Drops.*
2 John Surtees in 1965.
3 Argentina 1974.
4 None.
5 Graham Hill.
6 Niki Lauda and Jochen Rindt.
7 Emerson Fittipaldi.
8 F — Fangio = 5, Fittipaldi = 2 and Farina.

SCORE		
1st QUAL.		
2nd QUAL.		
RACE		
PITSTOP (1)		
PITSTOP (2)		
PITSTOP (3)		
PITSTOP (4)		
TOTAL		

SPAIN

FIRST QUALIFYING

1 ▲ Name this driver.

2 Who was the most successful pole position-winner of the 'seventies?

3 'Spiderman' helmet. Who?

4 Which team said goodbye to Formula One as a constructor in Adelaide in 1985?

5 What nationality is Oscar Larrauri?

6 Which venue, used only once for a Grand Prix, was called the Fair Park GP Circuit?

7 For how many teams has Jonathan Palmer driven: 3/4/5?

8 Who provides the English language commentaries at Grands Prix?

9 Where did Nigel Mansell enjoy his 100th Grand Prix start?

10 Which soft drink put a sparkle in Benetton in 1989?

11 How many fastest laps did Jim Clark set in his career: 16/23/28?

12 Where was Sandro Nannini's first rostrum finish?

13 Which is the only Grand Prix where practice begins on a Thursday?

14 What proportion of the race winner's total distance must cars have covered in order to be classified?

15 In which season did we last see a Grand Prix of Europe?

16 What is the minimum distance in metres, between the rows of a Grand Prix starting grid: 4/7/10? ▼

SECOND QUALIFYING

1 At which former World Championship circuit was there a section called Gants?

2 Of the drivers who have contested more than five races, who holds the highest percentage of wins?

3 At which circuit did some drivers opt for open-faced helmets in case they needed to throw up?

4 How many drivers drove for more than one team in 1989?

5 At which race did Stirling Moss claim the first of 16 pole positions?

6 The year is 1980, the car a Ligier, the number 25: who are we watching?

7 At which race did McLaren first use the TAG-Porsche turbo engine?

8 Who sponsored the Grand Prix of Europe at Brands Hatch in 1983?

9 Brabham won the 1985 French Grand Prix — giving whom their first victory since 1957?

10 Which was the only race Britain's Reg Parnell ever started from the front row? ▼

11 In 1986 Ken Tyrrell christened the select bunch of winning drivers the 'Gang of Five'. Who were the five?

12 In which year did Patrick Tambay take pole position — at his home Grand Prix?

13 Which race saw Derek Warwick on the rostrum for the first time?

14 True or false: Marc Surer, in his 82 races, was never on the rostrum?

15 Which driver gave the AGS Grand Prix car its first race?

16 Where and when did Niki Lauda secure his last pole position?

RACE DAY

1 Who designed the Shadow that took pole position on its first outing in 1975?

2 Which Brazilians finished 1-2 in their home race in 1975?

3 Graham Hill (seen here in Spain 1969) won the Monaco GP in which years? ▼

4 Who is the youngest driver to score World Championship points?

5 Which team, in 1977, won the first GP it entered?

6 When was the last time a German driver was on pole position?

7 Only three Italians have won the Italian GP: name them all.

8 Who designed the Motori Moderni V6 turbo engine?

9 An Arrows has only once been on pole. Where, when, who drove?

10 Which company supplied the tyres for the first-ever World Championship Grand Prix winner?

11 Who was the last man to win a Grand Prix at Clermont-Ferrand?

12 Peter Revson took only one pole position: where, when, in what?

▼

13 On only two circuits is the Grand Prix run anti-clockwise. Which?

14 Which driver was sacked at the 1989 Spanish GP — and saw his replacement have a massive accident?

15 At which race did Ayrton Senna score his first World Championship point?

16 Discounting Indianapolis, which driver boasts the highest percentage of victories in Grand Prix starts?

PIT STOP (1):

SPAIN

1 Name the two Barcelona circuits which have hosted the Spanish GP?

2 Why did the 1986 race go down in history?
▼

3 Who was the last driver to win at Jarama?

4 And the first?

5 Who was the first normally-aspirated finisher at Jerez in 1988?

6 Which driver won the Spanish Grand Prix in both 1977 and 1978?

7 In the 1989 race, which driver was higher on the grid than he had ever been before?

8 When did Jerez first stage the Spanish GP?

PIT STOP (2):

A YEAR IN FORMULA ONE: 1969

1 Jackie Stewart's first World Championship year. How many races did the Scot win?

2 He had two French team-mates in the course of the year. Who were they?

3 Graham Hill scored his last GP win. Where?

4 Jackie Ickx scored two wins — for whom?
▼

5 Every Championship race that year was won by a Ford Cosworth-engined car: true or false?

6 What unusual feature did the Lotus 63 and Matra MS84 share?

7 In one of the closest finishes ever, the first four cars were covered by less than two-tenths of a second. Where did this thrilling race take place?

8 Messrs Love and Lovely took part in the World Championship. Where were they from?

PIT STOP (3):

TEAM TALK: ALFA ROMEO

1 Which former Alfa Romeo engineer designed the Motori Moderni V6 engine used by Minardi?

2 Apart from Indianapolis, Alfa Romeo won every race in 1950 and were unbeaten in 1951 — until which event?
▼

3 Who had a one-off drive for Alfa Romeo in the 1950 British Grand Prix?

4 Alfa Romeo have been in and out of Formula One several times. In the 'seventies, how many years were they in?

5 How many victories have Alfa Romeo enjoyed?

6 What was the designation of the all-conquering Alfa Romeo of 1950?

7 An Alfa Romeo engine won two races in 1978 — but in the back of which car?

8 In 1979, when Alfa Romeo came back to Formula One after a 14-year absence, who drove for them?

PIT STOP (4):

RULES AND REGULATIONS

1 Which city houses the HQ of FISA?

2 Who won the last race of the 1.5 litre Formula in 1965?

3 What was the fuel limit on Turbo-charged cars in the last year of their existence in Formula Cne?

4 Apart from a medical centre, what other major medical piece of equipment has to be present before any official Formula One race or qualifying activity can take place?

5 For what offences were the Tyrrell team excluded from all results in the 1984 season?
▼

6 What is the maximum time limit for a Grand Prix?

7 In no circumstances may more than 26 cars start a GP — true or false?

8 What was the name ▶ of the Official Starter in the 1989 season?

RESULTS

FIRST QUALIFYING

1 Jean Alesi of France.
2 Niki Lauda.
3 Gabriele Tarquini.
4 Renault.
5 Argentinian.
6 Dallas, 1984.
7 Four: Williams/RAM/Zakspeed/Tyrrell.
8 Bob Constanduros.
9 Austria, 1987 — the same country where he made his debut.
10 7-up — one of their major sponsors.
11 Twenty-eight.
12 Silverstone 1988 (Benetton).
13 Monaco.
14 90%.
15 1985 — at Brands Hatch.
16 Seven.

SECOND QUALIFYING

1 Kyalami, South Africa.
2 Juan Manuel Fangio with 47.06%.
3 Clermont-Ferrand, France — its longest straight was one kilometre!
4 Six: Alboreto, Dalmas, Herbert, Raphanel, Gachot, Foitek.
5 British Grand Prix, 1955 (Mercedes).
6 Didier Pironi.
7 Dutch GP, Zandvoort 1983 in Niki Lauda's car.
8 John Player.
9 Pirelli tyres.
10 The very first World Championship GP — Great Britain 1950.
11 Prost/Rosberg/Senna/Mansell/Piquet.
12 French GP 1984 for Renault.
13 South African GP 1984 (third).
14 True: fourth (twice) was his best result.
15 Ivan Capelli (Italian GP 1986).
16 South Africa 1978 (Brabham).

RACE FOURTEEN

1 Tony Southgate.
2 Carlos Pace and Emerson Fittipaldi.
3 1963, '64, '65, '68 and '69.
4 Ricardo Rodriguez — 20 and 4 months at the 1962 Belgian GP (fourth).
5 Wolf — Argentina, thanks to Jody Scheckter.
6 1961 Italian GP — Von Trips.
7 Farina, Ascari, Scarfiotti.
8 Carlo Chitti.
9 Long Beach (USA West GP) 1981, Riccardo Patrese.
10 Pirelli.
11 Jackie Stewart (Tyrrell, 1972).
12 Canadian GP (Mosport), 1972, McLaren.
13 Brazil and Imola.
14 Christian Danner (Rial): the replacement was Gregor Foitek.
15 South Africa 1984 (sixth).
16 Juan Manuel Fangio, 24 wins in 51 races = 40.63%.

PIT STOP (1):

SPAIN

1 Pedralbes and Montjuich.
2 Senna's winning margin over Mansell was the closest ever (0.014 seconds).
3 Gilles Villeneuve (Ferrari 1981).
4 Graham Hill (Lotus 1968).
5 Nigel Mansell (Williams, 2nd).
6 Mario Andretti (Lotus).
7 Pierluigi Martini (Minardi, p4).
8 1986.

PIT STOP (2):

A YEAR IN F1 1969

1 Six.
2 Jean-Pierre Beltoise and Johnny Servoz-Gavin.
3 Monaco — where else?
4 Brabham.
5 True.
6 Four-wheel drive.
7 Monza, and Stewart won from Rindt, Beltoise and McLaren.
8 John Love was Rhodesian, Pete Lovely American.

PIT STOP (3):

TEAM TALK: ALFA ROMEO

1 Carlo Chiti.
2 British GP: Froilan Gonzales won in a Ferrari.
3 Reg Parnell.
4 One — 1979.
5 Ten — all in 1950-51.
6 Tipo 158.
7 Brabham, in Sweden and Italy.
8 Bruno Giacomelli and Vittorio Brambilla.

PIT STOP (4):

RULES AND REGULATIONS

1 Paris.
2 Richie Ginther (Honda, Mexico).
3 150 litres.
4 A helicopter.
5 They were alleged to have added ballast to their cars, and charged with fuel irregularities.
6 Two hours.
7 False; there have been many occasions even in recent times when 27 cars have started a Grand Prix.
8 Roland Bruynseraede.

SCORE		
1st QUAL.		
2nd QUAL		
RACE		
PITSTOP (1)		
PITSTOP (2)		
PITSTOP (3)		
PITSTOP (4)		
TOTAL		

JAPAN

FUJI TELEVISION
FUJI TELEVISION
Marlboro
Marlboro
Shell
Marlboro

FIRST QUALIFYING

1 Of what nationality is Robert Guerrero?

2 Which current Grand Prix circuit has a corner called Dry Sack?

3 Who is Team Williams most victorious Grand Prix driver ever?

▼

4 Which team recruited Bertrand Gachot's services when he was sacked by Onyx in 1989?

5 Which drivers — their surnames starting with the same letter — were involved in a major accident at Monaco in 1985?

6 What must every Grand Prix driver be able to do in a maximum of five seconds?

7 What was the record average speed set by Keke Rosberg in qualifying for the 1985 British GP?

8 How many times is a driver allowed to score points in World Championship races before he must start dropping scores?

9 True or false: the last driver to win a Grand Prix in his first season was Emerson Fittipaldi?

10 At which 1989 race did the popular Alex Caffi score his first-ever points?

11 Who were the 1984 Tyrrell drivers whose surnames began with the same initial?

12 Which famous driver was black-flagged at the 1986 Italian Grand Prix?

13 What was the nationality of Theodore and Toleman driver Johnny Cecotto?

14 Who is popularly nicknamed Steve Johnson?

15 Ayrton Senna has never won his national Grand Prix: true or false?

16 There have been World Championship Grands Prix in East London — but they weren't in England. How so?

SECOND QUALIFYING

1 At which 1984 race did Nigel Mansell incur a $6,000 fine for dangerous driving?

2 Did Innes Ireland ever win a Grand Prix?

3 Grand Prix racing visited Phoenix for the first time in 1989, and many people thought that was its first trip to a desert location. Not so: which other US venue was situated in California desert?

4 What, in Formula One, is Nomex?

5 Which German driver finished fourth — his only time in the points — in his national race in 1963?

6 Can you name this driver?
▼

7 Johnny Dumfries had one Grand Prix season. Which was the only round where he failed to qualify?

8 Britain's Brian Redman had just one rostrum finish in his 12 races. Where?

9 Who partnered Andrea De Cesaris in the Ligier line-up in 1984?

10 Who was the American who was Jackie Oliver's team-mate in Shadow's first season, 1973?

11 What was the last Grand Prix won by a Dunlop-shod car?

12 Cooper once provided the first four finishers in a Grand Prix. Which?

13 Which former British Grand Prix driver had the same name as a team manager who quit in 1989?

14 Two men incurred a one-minute penalty for jumping the start at the 1978 Italian GP — but for which one of them would have won?

15 Brazil 1981: Marc Surer gets fastest lap — in what car?
▼

16 At what point in a Grand Prix weekend does drivers' briefing take place?

RACE DAY

1 Which French driver in 1979 broke both legs in a hang-gliding accident?

2 Which former Ferrari, BRM and Honda driver died of cancer in 1989?

3 Why was the Theodore team so called? ▼

4 Which team won the 1954 French GP — its first-ever World Championship race?

5 Which current team manager set fastest lap in the 1968 Italian GP?

6 Who was the first driver to win the US and US (West) GPs in the same season?

7 Roy Salvadori was sixth in the British and Portuguese GPs of 1959 — in what make of car?

8 In which race did a Lyncar make its only GP start?

9 Most Grand Prix teams today have CAD/CAM systems. What do the initials stand for?

10 Ferrari, Osella and Coloni all have something in common, what? ▼

11 How was McLaren's victory in the 1989 Spanish GP a landmark in British Formula One history?

12 Which company's first GP car was designated 701?

13 Which team's car failed scrutineering on its first appearance, at Imola in 1988?

14 Why did Jackie Stewart's Tyrrell-Ford with chassis number 003 go down in history?

15 Which World Champion wrote an autobiographical volume called *Challenge Me the Race?*

16 What is the widest winning margin (in distance) in Grand Prix history?

PIT STOP (1):

JAPAN

1 How many Japanese GPs have there been? ▼

2 Who won the first?

3 Who retired from that race after only two laps?

4 Who won the second and last race at Fuji?

5 How did Williams win and lose in 1987?

6 What unique feat did Ivan Capelli achieve at Suzuka in 1988?

7 Four different teams have won a Japanese GP. Name them.

8 Which driver made his GP debut at Suzuka in 1987?

PIT STOP (2):

A YEAR IN FORMULA ONE: 1978

1 Two future World Champions made their Grand Prix debuts. Who and with which teams?

2 How many times was Mario Andretti on pole position?

3 Which driver scored his first Championship win — on home ground?

4 Who is this? ▼

5 Two teams scored just one point each. Which?

6 How many 1-2 finishes did Lotus score?

7 For which team did future World Champion Jody Scheckter drive?

8 It was the last year in which the World Championship visited a particular country and circuit. Which?

PIT STOP (3):

TRACK RECORD

1 Name this exclusive GP venue.

2 Station Hairpin is a famous corner — but what now stands in place of the station?

3 The track figured in the first World Championship but dropped out — to reappear when?

4 Which driver had his 50th GP there in 1987?

5 Two drivers have scored three consecutive wins: who?

6 When did Jackie Stewart first win there?

7 Which Briton scored his first ever points there in 1987?

8 The 1988 race saw one driver compete in his first GP. Who?

PIT STOP (4):

SPONSORS

1 Which team has raced under sponsorship from 33 backers calling themselves 'F1 Club'?

2 Name the three tobacco sponsors Team Lotus have had.

3 In 1970, who were the first sponsors of the March team?

4 Who sponsored the Graham Hill team in 1975?

5 Which sponsor left Shadow after the 1975 season?

6 What was unusual about Keke Rosberg's McLaren at the 1986 Portuguese GP?

7 How did John Surtees toy with the opposition in 1975?

8 What have Minardi's major 1989 sponsors in common with Ken Tyrrell?

RESULTS

FIRST QUALIFYING

1 Colombian.
2 Jerez, Spain — in the heart of sherry country.
3 Nigel Mansell with 13 wins.
4 Rial (at the Japanese GP).
5 Nelson Piquet (Brabham) and Riccardo Patrese (Alfa Romeo).
6 Get out of his cockpit with the steering wheel still in place.
7 160 mph — the first time it was ever achieved in a Formula One event.
8 Eleven.
9 True: both he and Clay Regazzoni did so in 1970, but Fittipaldi's was at the penultimate race, at Watkins Glen.
10 Monaco GP (Dallara, fourth).
11 Bellof and Brundle.
12 Alain Prost — for not respecting the start procedure.
13 Venezuelan.
14 Stefan Johansson.
15 True: second in 1986 in his best result in Brazil.
16 East London was the original venue for the South African GP.

SECOND QUALIFYING

1 US GP, Detroit (he started from the second row and tried to squeeze his Lotus between Prost's Renault and Piquet's Brabham.
2 Yes, USA 1961.
3 Riverside, scene of the 1960 race.
4 The trade name of the special fire-resistant material used in drivers' clothing.
5 Gerhard Mitter (Porsche).
6 Wolfgang Von Trips.
7 Monaco.
8 Jarama (Spain), 1968 in a Cooper-BRM.
9 François Hesnault (France).
10 George Follmer.
11 Belgian GP 1970 (Pedro Rodriguez, BRM).
12 French GP, 1960: Brabham — Gendebien — McLaren — Taylor.
13 Peter Collins.
14 Mario Andretti, whose Lotus was first across the line, and Gilles Villeneuve (Ferrari).
15 Ensign — the only time it achieved the feat.
16 One hour after the end of Sunday's warm-up.

RACE FIFTEEN

1 Patrick Depailler, who was lying third in the World Championship at the time.
2 Richie Ginther.
3 After its owner, Far East entrepreneur Theodore 'Teddy' Yip.
4 Mercedes-Benz, with Fangio at the wheel.
5 Jackie Oliver (Arrows) in a Lotus-Ford.
6 Carlos Reutemann (Ferrari) in 1978.
7 Aston Martin.
8 British GP 1975, John Nicholson driving.
9 Computer Aided Design/Computer Aided Manufacture.
10 Their first name; Enzo.
11 It took them past Lotus as the British team with most GP wins — 80 at that point.
12 March (1970).
13 Osella.
14 It scored eight race wins, to make it the most successful individual Formula One chassis.
15 Mike Hawthorn.
16 Jackie Stewart's Matra beat the McLaren of Bruce McLaren himself by two laps in the Spanish GP of 1969.

PIT STOP (1):

JAPAN

1 Five.
2 Mario Andretti.
3 Niki Lauda.
4 James Hunt.
5 Nigel Mansell hurt, Nelson Piquet World Champion.
6 He was the only normally-aspirated driver to lead a race in the year.
7 McLaren, Lotus, Ferrari and Benetton.
8 Roberto Moreno.

PIT STOP (2):

A YEAR IN F1 1978

1 Nelson Piquet, Ensign; Keke Rosberg, Theodore.
2 Eight.
3 Gilles Villeneuve for Ferrari in Montreal.
4 Patrick Depailler.
5 Surtees (Vittorio Brambilla sixth at Osterreichring); Ensign Derek Daly sixth in Montreal).
6 Four: Belgium, Spain, France, Holland.
7 Wolf.
8 Sweden, Anderstorp — Lauda won (Brabham Alfa).

PIT STOP (3):

TRACK RECORD

1 Monaco.
2 Loews Hotel.
3 1955.
4 Ayrton Senna.
5 Graham Hill and Alain Prost.
6 1966 BRM.
7 Jonathan Palmer.
8 Oscar Larrauri.

PIT STOP (4):

SPONSORS

1 Larrousse Calmels.
2 Gold Leaf, JPS and Camel.
3 STP (Scientifically Tested Products).
4 Embassy.
5 UOP (United Oil Products).
6 Instead of the usual red and white it was yellow and white, the colours of Marlboro Lights.
7 His cars were sponsored by Matchbox.
8 Timber — both were in the wood business.

SCORE		
1st QUAL.		
2nd QUAL.		
RACE		
PITSTOP (1)		
PITSTOP (2)		
PITSTOP (3)		
PITSTOP (4)		
TOTAL		

AUSTRALIA

WORLD
CHAMP SHIP
GOODYEAR
BARCLAY
DENIM
GOODYEAR
Canon
RENAULT
elf
BARCLAY
ICI
DENIM

FIRST QUALIFYING

1 Donington Park has never staged a World Championship Grand Prix: true or false?

2 What is Satoru Nakajima's best-ever finish?

3 Who is this?

▼

4 True or false: Jonathan Palmer has ever enjoyed a rostrum finish?

5 In 1984 Ferrari's solitary pole and single victory came at the same venue. Which?

6 Which engines did the Arrows team use in 1987 and 1988?

7 Benetton had both cars in the points twice in 1989: at which races?

8 Which current circuit is set out partly in a racecourse?

9 Who set fastest lap in the rain-soaked 1988 British GP?

10 In 1989, which driver scored his best result for three seasons but was later fired?

11 Where are Ferrari based?

12 Drivers from Great Britain had by the end of 1988 totalled 129 GP victories. From which country came the second highest total? France/Brazil/Italy.

13 Which team has a supporters' magazine called *Cobra*?

14 At which 1989 race did the Williams FW13 make its debut?

15 What is the number of cars allowed to take part in official practice at each race?

16 In which year did Camel assume sponsorship of Team Lotus?

SECOND QUALIFYING

1 When was the last Austrian GP?
▼

2 Name the Scottish driver who had his first Grand Prix at the British round in 1956.

3 True or false: Alain Prost is the only French driver whose race victories extend to double figures?

4 How many Grands Prix did Mario Andretti win in his World Championship year?

5 Two Frenchman monopolised the front row at Brands Hatch in 1980. Who?

6 Who was the unfortunate driver an irate Nelson Piquet tried to kick after their accident at Hockenheim in 1982?

7 Which vital element of a Grand Prix car must be at least 15 cm high and at least 3 cm thick.

8 Why was victory in the 1989 Italian Grand Prix especially significant for McLaren?

9 At which race did Coloni make their World Championship debut?

10 True or false: Thierry Boutsen has *never* started a Grand Prix from front row?

11 What distance is a Grand Prix expected to cover — in kilometres?

12 What was unusual about the 1985 British GP?

13 Alfa-Romeo took pole at the first ever World Championship Grand Prix. When was the last time?

14 Which current driver is nicknamed Poppy?

15 Who claimed a pole position in 1989 for the first time in six seasons?

16 Only once did a Hesketh set fastest race lap in 52 Grands Prix. Where, when?

RACE DAY

▲

1 OSCA was the name of a racing car firm founded in the early 'fifties by two brothers whose name was already famous in Grand Prix circles. What was their surname?

2 Kenny Acheson did well in the 1989 World Sportscar Championship, but how many Grands Prix did he contest in his brief Formula One career?

3 Everybody knows Nigel Mansell's first Formula One victory was in the 1985 Grand Prix of Europe at Brands Hatch. But who set fastest lap?

8 Which Anglo-Brazilian car achieved its best-ever result with second at the Brazilian GP of 1978?

9 Who was the former design henchman of Colin Chapman who died in 1989?

10 With which element of early World Championship racing car construction was the name De Dion associated?

11 What nationality was racing aristocrat Baron Emmanuel de Graffenried?

▼

12 Which team in 1989 saw both its drivers finish in the points at the same race for the first time?

13 Which circuit has hosted most World Championship GP?

14 Which pre-war Mercedes star was a guest driver for the same team in the 1954 German GP?

4 Which was the last Grand Prix victory for a supercharged — not turbocharged — car?

5 Which 1974 car was notable for its 'pyramid' sloping sides?

6 Why did Jackie Stewart miss the 1972 Belgian GP?

7 Britain's Trevor Taylor enjoyed a front-row start just once: where, when, for whom?

15 Which team holds the record for the number of fastest laps in a season?

16 Italian Nanni Galli drove in just one race for Ferrari: event and year, please?

PIT STOP (1):

AUSTRALIA

1 Who were the first sponsors of the Australian GP?

2 Three drivers went to Adelaide in 1986 with hopes of being World Champion. Who?

3 Victory in the inaugural Australian GP was the last for this driver. Who?

4 Name the long Adelaide straight.

5 Who made his debut for Williams at Adelaide in 1987?

6 Who was disqualified from second place in the 1987 Australian Grand Pix and why?

7 Which team scored its first-ever World Championship point at Adelaide in 1987?

▼

8 Who was the first driver to claim pole position in Adelaide?

PIT STOP (2):

A YEAR IN FORMULA ONE: 1988

1 Who was third in the Drivers' Championship behind Ayrton Senna and Alain Prost?

2 Who came third at Monza behind Berger and Alboreto?

3 What was Nigel Mansell's best result?

4 What record did Riccardo Patrese equal in Adelaide?

5 Who drove car number 31?

6 How many pole positions did Ayrton Senna claim?

7 Who deputised for the unwell Nigel Mansell at Spa?

▼

8 How many race laps did McLaren NOT lead: 16/28/41?

PIT STOP (3):

TEAM TALK: LIGIER

1 In which year did Ligier suffer their first non-qualification?

2 All Ligier cars start with the initials JS. Why?

3 What revolutionary feature marked the 1988 Ligier?

4 As a driver, in which car did Guy Ligier himself score a World Championship point in 1967?

5 Which two engines have powered Ligier to their eight wins?

6 Which was Ligier's most successful year?

▼

7 In which year did Ligier win the first two races of the season?

8 Laffite took six of Ligier's eight victories. Who scored the other two?

PIT STOP (4):

ENGINES

1 Probably the most famous engine in Grand Prix history is the Ford-Cosworth DFV? What does DFV stand for?

2 Which was the first World Championship victory for a rear-engined car?

3 When did a Honda-powered car score its first victory?

4 How many teams did John Judd supply with engines in his first year in Grand Prix racing?

5 Which was the first race in which a Hart-engined car raced?

6 On the TAG-Porsche engine, what did the initials TAG stand for?

7 How many Renault-engined victories, up to 1988, were *not* won by Renault cars?

▼

8 What was the engine in Dan Gurney's Eagle car named?

RESULTS

FIRST QUALIFYING

1. True.
2. Fourth, Silverstone 1987.
3. Gordon Murray.
4. True: the doctor's best result is fourth.
5. Zolder (Belgium) thanks to Michele Alboreto.
6. Megatron.
7. The first in Brazil and the last in Australia.
8. Adelaide, Australia.
9. Nigel Mansell (Williams-Judd).
10. Christian Danner, fourth at Phoenix, sacked in Spain by Rial.
11. Maranello, Italy.
12. France.
13. Brabham.
14. Portuguese GP — round 13!
15. Thirty.
16. 1987.

SECOND QUALIFYING

1. August 1987.
2. Ron Flockhart (BRM).
3. True: next is René Arnoux with 'only' seven.
4. Six (in 1978).
5. Didier Pironi and Jacques Laffite (both Ligier).
6. Eliseo Salazar of Chile.
7. Its race number.
8. They equalled Lotus as leading British team with 79 victories.
9. Spanish GP, 1987.
10. True.
11. Between 300 and 320.
12. An official's error led to the race being stopped a lap too soon.
13. 1982, USA West GP at Long Beach — De Cesaris driving.
14. Oscar Larrauri.
15. Riccardo Patrese (Williams) in Hungary.
16. Argentina, 1975.

RACE SIXTEEN

1. Maserati.
2. Just three between 1983 and 1985.
3. Jacques Laffite (Ligier) — the seventh and last of his career.
4. Spanish GP 1951: Fangio (Alfa Romeo) was the driver.
5. The Gordon Murray-designed Brabham BT44.
6. Because of a stomach ulcer.
7. Belgian GP at Spa-Francorchamps 1962 (Lotus Climax).
8. The Copersucar Fittipaldi driven by Emerson Fittipaldi.
9. Maurice Phillippe, who contributed to many of Chapman's Lotus designs.
10. It was a type of suspension system.
11. Swiss.
12. Minardi: Martini fifth, Sala sixth at the British GP.
13. Monza with 39 by the end of the 1989 Italian GP.
14. Hermann Lang.
15. Williams with 11 in 1986.
16. French GP 1972 — he finished 13th behind Jackie Stewart's Tyrrell.

PIT STOP (1):

AUSTRALIA

1. Mitsubishi.
2. Alain Prost, Nelson Piquet and Nigel Mansell.
3. Keke Rosberg.
4. Decquetteville Terrace.
5. Riccardo Patrese.
6. Ayrton Senna — illegal brake ducts on his Lotus.
7. AGS.
8. Ayrton Senna.

PIT STOP (2):

A YEAR IN F1 1988

1. Gerhard Berger.
2. Eddie Cheever.
3. Second at both Silverstone and Jerez.
4. 176 GP starts — same as G. Hill and Jacques Laffite.
5. Gabriele Tarquini (Coloni).
6. Thirteen.
7. Martin Brundle — he finished ninth.
8. Twenty-eight.

PIT STOP (3):

TEAM TALK: LIGIER

1. 1988.
2. To commemorate Guy Ligier's friend Jo Schlesser, killed in the 1968 French GP.
3. Its fuel tank was split into two sections.
4. Brabham.
5. Ford and Matra.
6. 1980: they scored 60 points and were second in the Constructors' Championship.
7. 1979, both by Jacques Laffite.
8. Patrick Depailler (Spain 1979) and Didier Pironi (Belgium 1980).

PIT STOP (4):

ENGINE

1. Double Four Valve.
2. Argentina 1958 (Cooper).
3. 1965, Mexico.
4. Three (March, Ligier and Williams).
5. Italian GP 1981 (Toleman).
6. Techniques d'Avant-Garde.
7. Five — all by Lotus 1985-6, and all by Senna.
8. Weslake.

SCORE		
1st QUAL.		
2nd QUAL.		
RACE		
PITSTOP (1)		
PITSTOP (2)		
PITSTOP (3)		
PITSTOP (4)		
TOTAL		